IN THE FOOTSTEPS OF JESUS

Five Attitudes

Louis-Marie Parent, O.M.I.

Translated by
Theresa Cademartori

Éditions Paulines

Originally published as *Sur les pas de Jésus* by Collection Volontaires de Dieu (Trois-Rivières, QC) in 1978, reprinted in 1985, 1989, 1990.

Also published in:

Spanish 1979, 1987, 1989
Italian 1986
Malayalam 1992

Cover: *Mike Lory*

Photo: *Jean-Jacques Gareau*

ISBN 2-89420-180-X

Legal Deposit — 3rd Quarter 1993
Bibliothèque nationale du Québec
National Library of Canada

© 1993 Collection Volontaires de Dieu
7535, boul. Parent
Trois-Rivières, QC, Canada
G9A 5E1

Éditions Paulines
250, boul. Saint-François Nord
Sherbrooke, QC, Canada
J1E 2B9

CONTENTS

Preface 7

Presence of God 9

  1. Definition of the Presence of God 10
  2. To Touch God Present within Us 16
    a) Presence of Immensity 16
    b) Presence of Friendship 18
  3. Qualities of the Presence of God 23
    a) Quality of Being 23
    b) Quality of Love 26
    c) Quality of Presence 29

Absence of Criticism 33

  1. Definition of Criticism 35
  2. The Damaging Effects of Criticism 43
  3. Advantages of the Absence of Criticism 49
  4. Unconditional Love of Our Neighbor 51
    a) Feelings 53
    b) Intelligence 54
    c) The Profound Richness of Our Being 55
  5. The Disinterested Encounter with Others . . . 57
    a) Love Our Enemies 57
    b) Let the Profound Love of Others
       Be Born in Us 60
    c) Let the Love of Others Grow in Us 61
    d) Protect Our Way of Loving Others 63

Absence of Complaint 67

  1. Terminology 68
  2. Definition of Complaint 72
  3. How Can We Avoid Complaint 76
  4. How Can We Fight Complaint 80
  5. Objective of the Absence of Complaint:
     Welcoming Events 83

Being of Service 91

  1. Terminology 92
    a) Being 92
    b) Service 95
    c) Beings of Service 96
  2. We Must Define Ourselves as Beings
     of Service 98
    a) The Voluntas Dei Institute 98
    b) The O.M.M.I.'s, and the Volunteers
      of God 100
  3. The Thought and Example of Jesus:
     a Being of Service 102
  4. We Are Invited to Model Our Lives
     on Jesus 108

Sower of Peace 113

  1. Terminology 114
  2. Definition of Peace 118
    a) What Peace Is Not 118
    b) What Peace Is 121
    c) Peace, a Fruit of Justice 123
    d) Peace, a Fruit of Love 124
  3. Requirements for Peace 128
  4. To Build Peace 132

Conclusion 137

PREFACE

Behold an invitation to march in the footsteps of Jesus. Who among us can pretend to listen to this call without hesitating: "*If anyone wishes to come after me, he must deny himself, take up his cross and follow me.*" (Lk 9:23) Such is the advice that stimulates the disciples of Christ.

Sanctity is not only for big heroes capable of performing fascinating actions; Jesus came for the salvation of everyone. Therefore, we must search the Gospels for a way of sanctity that is within reach of all persons of good will.

Father Louis-Marie Parent has dedicated his life to assisting his brothers and sisters to build their lives on Gospel principles, to meet the Lord and to learn to love him. To do this he has continually meditated the Gospels:

> "Not everyone who says to me, 'Lord, Lord,' will enter the kingdom of heaven, but only the one who does the will of my Father in heaven. ... Everyone who listens to these words of mine and acts on them will be like a wise man who built his house on rock." (Mt 7:21-24)

In order to form the attitudes of Jesus within us, Father Parent, through the inspiration of the Holy

Spirit, succeeded in drawing up five concrete points to be lived in our daily situations and encounters. *The presence of God, the absence of criticism, the absence of complaint, being of service, to be a sower of peace*: here we have a solid spirituality. These five points are a proven road which lead us towards the Father in the footsteps of Jesus. By the pontifical approval of Secular Institutes, the Oblate Missionaries of Mary Immaculate and the Institute Voluntas Dei, and by the approval of their constitutions, the Church has given this spirituality a twofold recognition.

Thanks to the diligence of the members of these two Institutes and of the associate group, the Volunteers of God, thousands of persons in different countries have adopted this program of life.

Moreover, and this was always of prime importance to the author, these five points are within reach of all: try them and see.

This book is an invitation to advance, step by step, in the reality of the present moment. You are secure, the Lord will take you by the hand. Go forward: have a good journey!

Mario Laroche
Ex-Director General
Voluntas Dei Institute

Presence of God

It is not easy to give a definition of the *presence of God.* Nor is it easy to give a definition of our presence to God. However, certain descriptions can help clarify these two states: God in my presence and I in His.

God is always present to me as Creator, Providence and Father, and all is present to God. Nothing escapes him, neither in my being, my thoughts, nor my activities, neither in my imagination, my dreams, nor my sentiments. All my desires are known to him. Even in the most secret corners of my mind, he is able to detect all my unruly sentiments as well as those that are agreeable and calm. He is the attentive witness to each instant of my existence. He knows everything: when I sit or when I stand; when I walk, when I run or when I waste time. He is constantly present; tirelessly he gazes at me with the same expression of goodness. He is more present to my life than I am to my own thoughts. He is never distracted; his eye is fixed on me, I am the best qualified subject of his mercy. Nothing in my life surprises him, nothing repulses him. He is slow to anger, patient and faithful to his covenant. He knows how to wait, because love never tires.

1. Definition of the Presence of God

Thomas a Kempis, author of *The Imitation of Christ* (Book 3, chap. 4, v. 1), gives a descriptive definition of the *presence of God* and of his own personal efforts to be attentive to God: to stand before God, to walk in his presence, to keep watch over my motivations and to act from supernatural motives. To live in the presence of God is to be recollected, to pay heed to the Lord living within me. It is to listen to him speaking in me through my conscience, my aspirations, through persons and events.

The Imitation of Christ calls happy those who habitually turn towards God, who take time to prepare their hearts to listen to him. Happy are those who hear the Lord speaking in the depths of their being; happy are those who receive words of consolation from the mouth of the Lord. Happy the attentive ears that listen not to exterior voices but to the truth that lives within them. Happy are those who penetrate the mysteries preserved in their hearts and who, by daily exercises, prepare themselves more and more to understand the secrets of heaven. Happy are those who find their joy in serving God. Happy are those who close the door to dissoluteness and who listen to the word of God — the inner inspiration.

Only faith can incite us to remain in the *presence of God.* Even if the world does not succeed in completely gratifying us, nevertheless, it is so interesting, so captivating. It is quite efficacious in corroding our lives and gnawing away at our time. Without realizing it enough, we become slaves of the world, and our precipitous rhythm wears down our capacity for reflection. As we let ourselves be devoured by the attractions of the world, we become incapable of discerning between an efficacious good, namely the formation of the Christian, and an immediate good, namely one that is superficial, transitory and often insidious.

To remain in the *presence of God,* we must recognize his omnipresence. Faith teaches us that God is in objects, in events, and in persons, that he is wherever good takes root and subsists. We must also discover God in ourselves. He is a living, acting, loving Being eager to contact us and to enter into dialogue with us.

To live in the *presence of God* is to habitually use whatever is at hand to discover Him everywhere. Jesus says to his first companions:

> "Look at the wild flowers of the field. They do not work nor spin. But I tell you that not even Solomon in all his splendor was clothed like one of them. If God so clothes the grass of the field which grows today and is thrown into the oven tomorrow, will he not much more provide for you, O you of little faith?" (Mt 6:28-30)

> "Look at the birds in the sky; they do not sow nor reap; they gather nothing into barns, yet your heavenly Father feeds them. Are you not more important than they?" (Mt 6:26)

To live in the *presence of God* is to develop the aptitude of turning to God at all times and in all places. If God lives in us, why do we not think of him more often? Let us realize that the Lord always gives us first place in his scheme of things. We must believe that he considers all human beings superior to flowers and animals. What he does for these latter, he will surely do for us in order to encourage our progress.

God paid dearly for our friendship; the price: the blood of his Son. Thus, he is not satisfied with merely holding first place in our hearts, *he wants all of us.* He wants to be in control of our very being; the choice of what a human heart can contain belongs to him. He desires to act in his own way; he wants each human being to become docile to his will. Still, God does not want to do violence to us. For our own good, he wants us to understand what he accomplishes by remaining present to us and by following us everywhere with his goodness and his mercy. If we could only understand!

The *presence of God* has the power to maintain our whole being in good, to bind our passions, to direct our affections, to channel our sentiments, to determine the rhythm of our friendships, to develop in our hearts spirit, ardor and vitality, and to help us to support the hard knocks of life.

The *presence of God* enables us to follow the example of Jesus, to be grafted onto the Father and turned toward our neighbor. It opens our mind to a better knowledge of God, stimulates love, sows enthusiasm and keeps our hearts alert.

The *presence of God* is a school where we are taught to love. It is a technique that awakens us and permits us to joyfully discover in things, events and persons a multitude of little presences of God: in ourselves, in others, in nature, everywhere.

The *presence of God* is an awareness that the Holy Spirit is in us, that he lives, acts, loves and inspires us to accomplish positive deeds, as the Gospels so often demonstrate.

"*Now there was a man in Jerusalem whose name was Simeon. ... the holy Spirit was upon him. It had been revealed to him by the holy Spirit that he would not see death until he had seen the Messiah of the Lord. He came into the Temple moved by the Spirit.*" (Lk 2:25-27) The presence of God is a recognition that the Holy Spirit abides within me, that he speaks to me and moves me. That is why old Simeon had the greatest joy of his life, that of holding the Infant-God in his arms.

An elderly woman named Anna had no other interest in the world except God. She never left the temple; she served God night and day in prayer and fasting. (cf. Lk 2:36-37) She, too, received the joy of touching the Infant-God.

The awareness is important; in fact, it is indispensable, because we can be in God's presence without ever discovering him.

The adolescent Jesus was in Jerusalem. He was in the temple in the midst of the doctors. They looked at him, admired him, found him intelligent, even brilliant. (cf. Lk 2:46) All the same, none of them saw the Messiah in this child prodigy because none of them were attuned to the Holy Spirit.

13

These intellectuals simply considered the presence of Jesus on a rational basis.

He who seeks the Lord wants for no good thing, says the psalmist. (Ps 34:11) Jairus, one of the synagogue officials, often stands in the presence of God. His daughter is dying and he is ready to do anything to save her life. The doctors do not understand her illness. He hastens to Jesus, drops to his knees and pleads earnestly: "*My daughter is at the point of death. Please, come lay your hands on her that she may get well and live.*" (Mk 5:23) The daughter dies but Jesus raises her from the dead.

A woman afflicted with hemorrhages for twelve years has visited all the doctors possible. She spent all her money without being healed. She believes in Jesus: "*...if I could just draw near to him, if I could touch the hem of his garment, I will be healed.*" She is in the presence of Jesus; she walks up to him, touches his cloak (a gesture of faith) and feels well. Jesus turns around and demands to know who touched him. The Apostles intervene — many people have touched you. But Jesus answers: "*I felt a power go out of me.*" The woman in fear and trembling tells him the truth and gives witness to him. Jesus says to her: "*Daughter your faith has saved you. Go in peace and be cured of your affliction.*" It has been confirmed; the change that she felt within herself was her healing. (Mk 5:25-34)

To live in the *presence of God* is to be attentive to God, his wisdom, power, goodness and mercy. It is to believe in him to the point of folly, to pray by looking at someone with the eyes of the heart. It is

14

to wait, to believe, and to receive with thanksgiving the gift of faith.

To remain in the *presence of God* is to seek him like the disciples of Emmaus. They were walking along the road that led away from Jerusalem. A stranger drew near and walked with them. They were visibly sad and he empathized with their grief. They felt themselves moved by the healing words of this man who was so well-versed in Holy Scripture. They invited him to spend the evening with them, and they recognized him in the breaking of the bread...

Mary Magdalene sought Jesus... where had they laid him? She found him and did not recognize him. Jesus called her by name and Mary wanted to throw herself into his arms.

The situation of the disciples of Emmaus and of Mary Magdalene demonstrates that if we allow ourselves to be grafted onto God by placing ourselves in his presence, our seeking will result in our discovering him. He will give us a sign so that we, too, can recognize him. There will be a "breaking of the bread" where we will hear him call our name. He knows us so well; he loves us so dearly.

Let us get used to remaining in the presence of God, to becoming aware of his presence. This is essential for every spiritual journey. Jesus tells us "...*no one can come to the Father except through me. I am the Way.*" (Jn 14:7)

2. To Touch God Present within Us

a) *Presence of Immensity*

God created man in his image and likeness. (Gn 1:26) God is therefore our Creator and also our Providence and Defender. As the author of life, God exercises a *presence of immensity* over us, giving us life, but also preserving it. He places a static force in each of us that enables us to stand firm and to resist, but also a dynamic force that permits us to subsist, to progress, to evolve, and to establish a relationship with him.

Therefore, God has placed his own powers in each human being, without any danger of his becoming poorer. We will thus find within ourselves the riches that exist in God and if we can find them in ourselves, we can also find them in others whether or not they are aware that they possess these riches. Their attitude changes nothing as far as God is concerned.

God is so present in us, so identified with our lives, that if he were to withdraw, life would be annihilated. God is not only the principle of life but also the principle of its conservation, of its duration, and its progress. God is the Creator who both gives life and distributes its positive qualities: our natural talents, our gifts, our aptitudes, our energies, our dynamism; the powers to love, to understand, to be free, and to have confidence. All these give us a personality, a free will, a proper and distinct identity, an unchangeable autonomy, an irresistible empathy. If God gave us all this gratuitously without demanding our collaboration, it is because he does not expect us to return the favor.

All is freely given, and God, through his Providence, continues his work by preserving what he has made, by placing at our disposal all the defense mechanisms needed that we need to protect ourselves against disintegration, aging, the hard knocks of life, and the toxins of suffering accumulated in our interpersonal relationships. He gives us natural life because he is the Creator; he preserves it because he is Providence.

Whoever we are, Providence watches over us. This goodness on the part of God does not depend on our mood, on our degree of understanding nor on our collaboration. Whether we practice our faith or not, whether we are atheists or unbelievers, whether we are indifferent, oblivious, tepid, slothful and treacherous, or fervent and committed to his service, we will enjoy the same benefits, the same temperature, the same gardens and have the right to the same measuring stick. Our efforts will be rewarded according to the use we make of our intelligence and will. The sun shines on everyone; rain falls on all doorsteps; cold penetrates all walls; heat effects every person because all of us, without exception, are made in the image and likeness of God.

b) *Presence of Friendship*

There is also another form of the presence of God, the *presence of friendship*. This is given to us on the day of our baptism and presupposes our adhesion to it as soon as we are able to reason. On the day of our confirmation, it continues its development insofar as we do our part. It does not function without our collaboration.

By baptism, all the natural powers received at birth acquire an indescribable, supernatural vigor. Baptism creates in us an unfathomable mystery: God has accepted as his child the one that he created in his image. God, the divine artist, desires to adopt his handiwork and to insert it into his own divine life!

Confirmation, which is consciously requested, awakens us to this form of presence where God makes us his own children, loves us as a father, and produces marvels in us by the power of his Spirit who has chosen us to become his Temples.

The Holy Spirit is in us. He delivers himself into our hands, his mission is to make us witnesses of Christ. He allows us to use all his gifts for as long as we want to utilize them. He fills us with abundant charisms; he nourishes us with his fruit. His table is always plentiful, he gives us abundant fruit. Holy Scripture enumerates some of them for us: love, peace, joy, patience, kindness, generosity, faithfulness, gentleness, self-control. (cf. Gal 5:22) Because we are children of God, we only have to help ourselves to whatever we want. In this way God strives to make us feel like one of the family.

If the *presence of immensity* acts without our collaboration, the *presence of friendship* works only in rhythm with our cooperation. All the riches belonging to a child of God are within us, but they are absolutely without effect, if we do not believe in their value. However, if we adhere to Christ, they can have considerable creativity: if we strive to live in his spirit, in his style, and if we establish here on earth a positive relationship with his Father.

Thus we must become aware of God's presence of friendship in each of us. We must be convinced of the necessity of faith, as Jesus taught us more than once. If you believe in me, if you are baptized, if you observe my commandments, you will have eternal life and my Father will live in you as he lives in me, and I shall be in you as I am in the Father. (cf. Jn 15)

God is the principle of positive action. He sanctifies us, possesses our being and transforms it. God not only knows all our problems but he also has on hand the best solution for each of them. He requires our collaboration: not simply an exercise of asceticism to prove our love for him through renunciations, but simply an attitude, a gesture from the heart, an act of faith. He asks us to believe in the love that he brings us, to believe that we are loved by him, that we are precious in his sight, that we are a part of his plan, that he is present in us, that nothing in us escapes his goodness and his mercy.

We must believe that if we allow him the liberty of loving us, he will guide us, sanctify us and lead us out of our anguish, our anxieties and our problems. He does not want to make us slaves who become pliable because they are constantly threatened but free persons who have been paid for and redeemed by the blood of Jesus. (cf. Gal 3:26) He wants us to be proud like children, without being arrogant. He wants us to walk with our heads held high, our hearts free, like someone willingly engaged in serving an infinitely loving Father, who has freely chosen us to become the object of his predilections because we are his children, his sons and daughters.

God takes the responsibility for animating us, for activating us. He asks us to look upon him with faith, with a positive, confident attitude. We must feel that we are loved; we must get used to letting him act, to watching him do things, to letting him bring about changes in us that give him pleasure. God is the active agent of our perfection, he wants us to remain passive under his gaze of friendship. We receive all from him; our role consists in showing him our gratitude, in manifesting to him our joy and in being happy.

We must have the same confidence as St. Paul had when he wrote to the Romans:

"What will separate us from the love of Christ? Will anguish, or distress, or persecution or famine, or nakedness, or peril, or the sword? ... No, in all these things we conquer overwhelmingly through him who loved us. For I am convinced that neither death, nor life, nor angels, nor principalities, nor present things, nor future things, nor powers, nor height, nor depth, nor any other creature will be able to separate us from the love of God in Christ Jesus our Lord." (Rom 8:35-39)

To believe that I am loved by God is to believe that God has a plan for my life, and that he has already foreseen the means of accomplishing it. It is to believe that I have been chosen to be his instrument in the realization of this plan. But I must allow myself to be possessed and gripped by Christ, without counting the cost.

Wherever we are, there are vibrations. If I have a television set, I capture images and sounds. But these vibrations hide many riches from our senses. God, too, is in the atmosphere. It is up to us, through our attentiveness and vigilance, to discover him, to gaze upon him, to listen to him. Our attention is the instrument that detects God there where he is. The heart of our attention is the thought that God loves us, that he has done everything for us, that he is constantly leaning over us by his *presence of immensity* and his *presence of friendship*.

When God takes hold of a heart, it suddenly becomes fascinated by him and totally abandons itself into his hands. It is no longer concerned with itself; only God counts. To love God for himself alone, to love him in everything and everywhere: in nature, events, people, and in oneself, is to receive from God the most beautiful vocation in the world. It is to fulfill the most wonderful mission on earth. This love will grow insofar as I am conscious of what he accomplishes in me, for me, by me, so that I may be transformed in him. His action in me is awesome, but it is just as beautiful in those whom I call my neighbors. Therefore, it is up to me to discover in others these *presences of God, presences of friendship.* God unites us in his love when we seek to understand his manner of loving, absorbing, assimilating, and unifying.

It would be good to stop and to analyze with our hearts what it is we feel within ourselves when we feel loved by God. What is the quality of the relationship that unites us to him? It is not fear, but friendship, love, abandonment, confidence, a need to be faithful, to correspond to his sentiments.

We strongly perceive within ourselves the desire not to grieve the Lord, but to accomplish all that is pleasing to him. We feel the need to meet with him in the depths of our being. When we become aware that we are God's temples, that we are truly his children, that we belong to the family of God, that he takes pleasure in each of us because he finds himself in all that is agreeable, then we can feel that we have succeeded before God. He alone is the universal author of all good and of each individual good.

Our life will be a failure if we pass God by. If we only seek God occasionally, we will lack happiness here on earth. We must become aware that God is someone alive, active and loving, someone who lives in the heart of our being, so that he becomes the totality of our lives.

It would be good for each of us to write the story of our spiritual life, to note the important moments where we were moved by the goodness of God. This story is alive in the depths of our heart. A few hours of recollection and we will rediscover those moments when the presence of God filled us with enthusiasm. We have lived hours of spiritual euphoria. These marvelous moments appear in different forms. In the lives of St. Paul, St. Augustine, the venerable Libermann, Blessed Eugene de Mazenod and Charles de Foucauld, they took on the aspect of conversion. In the lives of St. John of the Cross and St. Teresa of Avila they appeared as a desire for reform, a desire for a more precise and conscious contact with God.

God is always ready to appease our hunger and our thirst.

3. Qualities of the Presence of God

God created us in his image and likeness. He wanted us to truly become his own children. To become children of God it is necessary to have real values. He himself gives them to us; it is up to us to make them fructify by paying special attention to three qualities: *the quality of being, the quality of presence, and the quality of love.*

a) *Quality of Being*

A human being is of great importance in the eyes of God. In ancient times, Moses almost went into ecstasy at the thought of God's attention for us.

"God protects each person who belongs to his people. He shields them and cares for them, guarding them as the apple of his eye. As an eagle incites its nestlings forth by hovering over its brood, so he spread his wings to receive them and bore them up on his pinions." (Dt 32:10-11)

David also was filled with enthusiasm when he wrote:

"What is man that you should be mindful of him or the son of man that you should care for him? You have made him little less than the angels and crowned him with glory and honor. You have given him rule over the works of your hands, putting all things under his feet... O Lord, our Lord, how glorious is your name over all the earth!" (Ps 8: 5-8,10)

God knows the value of human beings because he is their Creator. Like God, let us try to discover the richness of our being by evaluating the qualities, gifts, talents, energies, and vitality that he deposits in each of us. If we think of these values as gifts of God, we will strengthen our ability to concentrate, not only on the power of God but on his mercy, his goodness, and his wisdom. Thus it is not a matter of coming before God and presenting him with our foolishness, our stupidities, our blunders and our sins. This state of mind must last only for as long as it takes to ask pardon. Rather, we must approach God by using the paths that lead directly to him: these paths are our qualities.

Each lived quality is rooted in our being and is a sample of an attribute of God. These qualities are the abilities which God places in those whom he has chosen as his instruments to carry out his plan of creation. God asks each of us to become aware of our qualities, to believe in them, to live them. He invites each of us to be ourselves. He incites us to realize the positive riches that he has deposited in us. It is by means of our qualities that we establish a true relationship with the Father who made us temples of his Holy Spirit. Qualities are truly the pathways that lead us to the heart of the Father and to deepest intimacy with him.

The *presence of God* is an awareness of the gifts received from God in the form of energies, capacities, and dynamisms. This awareness must create optimism and enthusiasm in us if it is to transform our lives.

The *presence of God* signifies being lucid, realizing that God is there in the depths of our being and that we must allow him to live. It is to recognize that we participate in the very life of God, that we belong to him, that our qualities are expressions of him, that our gifts and our talents are samples of his own attributes, that we become human presences of God in our milieu.

The *presence of God* is nourished by prayer and develops through the admiration He provokes in us by His works. We can say with David: "*The Lord is... holy in all his works. The Lord is near to all who call upon him... He fulfills the desire of all who fear him... He keeps all who love him...*" (Ps 145:18-20)

Let us place ourselves in the presence of God with all the qualities and gifts we have received from him. We must recognize the fact that we belong to him, that we come from him, that we remain his. Our wretchedness can also be an occasion for going to him, but as the parable of the vine and the branches explains, if we are grafted onto him, we will receive the sap that vivifies the branches. For each of us, the sap means the natural qualities that we received at birth and the riches of the grace received in baptism. And, the day we feel a call in our hearts to follow him into a relationship of intimacy, we will have the assurance that we are on the right road, on the right path.

God is interested in us; we belong to him; we have our origins in him; our subsistence depends on him. He is our support, our strength, our refuge, our rock. He is always faithful to his covenant. His love is perfect. Perfect love touches all the fibers of one's being; it does not let go. This love is perfect in quality, intensity, immensity, and duration.

It is our being as it has come from the hands of our Creator that attracts and calls forth his goodness and mercy. (cf. Jn 17:26; Rom 5:5)

b) *Quality of Love*

I can love God in two ways: for his gifts and for what he is.

To love God for his gifts. I can attach myself to God, not leaving him for one instant, being constantly at his heels, because I am weak, my needs are numerous, my way of obtaining what I believe is necessary are limited. Moreover, as we see in the Gospel accounts, the Lord lends himself well to this kind of prayer since he says that he has come to save what was lost, and he invites us into solitude to speak to our hearts. He invites us to rest in him, and he promises to answer all that we ask the Father in his name.

I turn to him because he gives me security, he takes care of my needs, he makes my life interesting. He gives me a foretaste of the hundredfold that he promised. I know that he is there to help me in the sufferings and trials inherent in life and that he will not abandon me in difficult moments. He is always there present. I know him well enough to know that he is faithful to his commitments. He is a friend whom I can count on in the least difficulty. I know that I can constantly keep my eye on him, that he will respond to my needs. It is truly impossible to find someone who gives me a greater sense of security. (cf. Jn 14:10-12; 15:5-7)

To love God for who he is. I can convince myself that God is Father, and that God is love, that he wants to be loved for himself because he is peace, joy, kindness, goodness, gentleness, tenderness, amiability, mercy, patience, and fidelity, equanimity and strength; he is the perfect master of himself. He wants me to go to him always. He has chosen me from all eternity. He sends his Son and his Holy Spirit to dwell in me:

"The Word was made flesh and dwelt among us."
(Jn 1:14)

"But when the Spirit of truth comes, he will guide
you in all truth. He will not speak on his own, but
he will speak what he hears, and will declare to
you the things that are coming. He will glorify
me, because he will take from what is mine and
declare it to you." (Jn 16:13-14)

"I am the vine, you are the branches. Whoever
remains in me and I in him will bear much fruit,
because without me you can do nothing." (Jn
15:5)

"As the Father loves me, so also I love you.
Remain in my love." (Jn 15:9)

Jesus wants to inaugurate in each of us his
kingdom that has existed from all eternity. (cf. Col
1:19; 2:9) He wants to construct in us a solid city.
(cf. Heb 11:10) He wants to be the only foundation
of our spiritual life. He is anxious for us to build
upon him alone. (cf. 1 Cor 3:11) Jesus desires just
one thing: to be one with us.

In this exchange with God, it is no longer we
who take the initiative, it is he. We no longer seek
our own interests but rather we endeavor to know
him, to love him and to serve him. We try to learn
from his example. We trust him; we do not speak
to him about ourselves but about him; we listen as
he tells us about himself. This way is better, it is
more relaxed, our love is more single-minded.
Besides stimulating an awareness of his presence

living, acting and loving in me, this love also brings about an unconditional surrender, a sense of abandonment that enables us to say with Abraham in the most mysterious difficulties: God will take care of it.

When we have attained this degree of self-giving, we will discover God well-rooted in us, and our dialogue with him will be easier, deeper, and more natural. We will feel all our faculties unified by him and we will become one with him: what joy, what fruit, what love!

c) *Quality of Presence*

God is always there, his presence is permanent, but he is discreet, he awaits our invitation. As soon as we turn towards him, he shines his light of friendship on us. As soon as we pay attention to him, he becomes all ours. He has the power to do many things at once; he can respond to all the expressions of my love. To be present: that is the quality that he possesses perfectly. He is the eternal Present, eternal Life, eternal Action, eternal Lover. We can say that when we pay attention to him he becomes all ours. He has nothing else to do. He respects our liberty, he knows how to wait because he is Love. To develop a grand intimacy with him, we must survey *our quality of being, our quality of loving and our quality of presence.*

Our *quality of being* is, in reality, the wealth of our own personality as it has come forth from the hands of the Creator and been deified in the blood of Christ.

Our *quality of loving* is our capacity to establish a stable and durable relationship with God the Father who, because of the generosity of his Son, Jesus Christ, graces us with the presence of the Holy Spirit, who lives in us and guides us as long as we allow it.

Our *quality of presence* is our attitude of abandonment which helps us to break away from all that distracts us in order to plunge us into the will of the Father. This Father always has an eye on us which we call our conscience.

All of us should decide to live a profound relationship with God. The *presence of God* is not only the foundation of all spiritual life, of every serious spiritual journey towards God but it is also the mystique which permits an image of God to turn toward its Creator, a likeness of God to seize the benefits of Providence, a child of God to be inserted into the family of the Trinity. Moreover, it is our raison d'être, our special charism, because it is the mission that we have received from the Church: to be sowers and builders of peace.

We will succeed in living this vocation if we reflect on the daily means that are offered us by the Holy Spirit. Why not try to gain a better knowledge of the qualities that dwell within us? Why not practice living one or other of these qualities each day? Thus we would develop a capacity for concentration, a growing taste for spiritual things, and an intense desire to belong totally to God.

We have qualities in us which can be summed up by enumerating the theological and moral virtues and the fruits of the Spirit: faith, hope, charity, prudence, justice, strength, temperance, love, peace, joy, kindness, gentleness, patience, faithfulness, and self-control. Each 24 hours we promise the Lord to live one or other of these virtues or qualities. Thus we strive to concentrate on one of the strong points of our being, we are sure to live according to the mind of God and we dispose ourselves to receive the abundance of blessings that he reserves each day for those who live in his love.

I close this chapter by saying to you what Jesus said to a doctor of the Law after placing him on the road of love: Do this and you will live. I am going to take this advice; why don't you also take it?

Absence of Criticism

God has a plan for us: he wants us to love him above all else and to love our neighbor as ourself. It is not easy to love because, by nature, love is an absolute and does not accept half measures. Love demands that we go to the limits of our strength, into the depths of our being to find there the qualities, gifts, talents and energies that are its usual expressions. Without searching for the richness constituted by our personality, we will never reach true and authentic love.

Love goes beyond the impulses of passion, sexual drives or the volcanic sentiments of sudden, emotional affection. True love is God within us welcoming or visiting God in the other.

By birth each of us becomes an image and likeness of God. (cf. Gn 1:26) By baptism and faith all become children of God. Therefore God has predisposed, established and regulated within us all the powers necessary to love. We also have additional capacities which God distributes to those whom he has chosen to be his children, along with Jesus whom he considers "the firstborn". All these powers, sown in profusion in the human being, become instruments of love. Our strengths are innumerable and extraordinary; they make us marvels in the eyes of God.

To accomplish the plan of God is to live the best of ourselves each day. To live the best of ourselves is to carry out God's plan for us. God is both Love and the Sower of Love as well as its Great Distributor. Paul of Tarsis tells his disciple Timothy: "*He saved us and called us to a holy life not according to our works but according to his own design and the grace bestowed on us in Christ Jesus before time began.* (2 Tm 1:9)

Our vocation on earth is to live love; it is to allow others to speak to us of love; it is to welcome love and to spread it to those around us. Love has *three levels of perfection*:

The first is to treat others as we treat ourselves, to love one another as we love ourselves. (cf. Jn 13:34) "*Do to others whatever you would have them do to you.*" (Mt 7:12)

The second level is to love others as Jesus loved us. (cf. Jn 15:12) "*My little children, I will not leave you orphans... I will send you the Paraclete, the Consoler.*" (Jn 14:18; 16:7) The summit of love is to give our lives for those we love. (cf. Jn 15:13) That is what Jesus did for us to procure salvation for us.

The third level is to love one another as the Father loves the Son. "*This is my beloved Son with whom I am well pleased; listen to him.*" (Mt 17:5)

God established a plan of love in which he does not tolerate weakness. He wants us to reach for the heights; there are no risks to take, there are no wasted efforts. The great risk that can stop us from attaining this love is *destructive criticism* which

34

makes us destroyers. Destroyers are incapable of profound love; they lose sight of God's plan and seek imitations of love wherever they see it be it in emotivity, or in the dissoluteness of their passions. We see them running from deception to deception, their mouths twisted in bitterness..

Let us endeavor to describe *destructive criticism*, and the damage it causes, and try to find out how God wants each of us to behave toward our neighbor. We must know the definition of destructive criticism if we want to avoid it in order to protect our love of God and neighbor, and to consider the presence of God as the most important means of remaining faithful to our Christian vocation.

1. Definition of Criticism

We can give many different meanings to the word *criticism*. The dictionary gives this meaning to *constructive criticism*: it is the study of a principle or a fact in order to make a judgement, an appreciation from the aesthetic or philosophical point of view. We also say that it is an intellectual or moral judgement, the study of the positive values of someone. In reality this criticism is an objective, positive appreciation of a person, their works, or their actions. This type of criticism is praiseworthy and beneficial; we should all encourage it and exercise it.

On the other hand, *destructive criticism* is completely different. It is a cancer that devours a reputation right down to its roots, like the larva of certain butterflies which at times destroy the pine forests of Quebec. Up to the present, no one has managed to describe adequately the intensity or immensity of the damage caused. Or could destructive criticism be "*the roaring lion seeking to devour?*" (cf. 1 Pt 5:8-9)

This criticism is an unfavorable judgement made about someone without a reason, without a motive, without the right. It is the manifestation of discontent in regard to someone, absent or present, but whose identity is usually known. It is an unfavorable judgement made about someone when we look at their negative side.

In *destructive criticism* we emphasize a scandal, be it a calumny or a rash judgement. This criticism is caused by an impulse of pride, a wounded susceptibility, an uncontrolled sensuality or a poorly restrained aggressiveness. This type of criticism has existed since the beginning of time. All of us have experienced it during the course of our lives, either by criticizing or by being the target of criticism.

In his first book of *The Imitation of Christ* (paragraph 16), Thomas a Kempis gives ordinary Christians some wise advice to help make life in society supportable.

"What we cannot correct in ourselves or others we must support with patience until the Lord changes things... Strive to patiently support the faults and infirmities of others whatever they may be because you also give others many things to endure. If you are not able to become what you would like to be, how can you change others according to your desires?... If you are incapable of changing yourself, how can you pretend to change others?"

Thomas a Kempis invites us to stop dreaming and to be realistic; in paragraph 14 he had already written:

"By judging others, we tire ourselves uselessly; we more often err and commit many faults, but by examining ourselves and judging ourselves we can bring forth much fruit."

In the face of criticism, we must either be silent or change the topic of conversation as if we had not understood anything. We must avoid getting caught up in such an explosive subject. A good sign of love of neighbor is to refuse to criticize; it is to respond to criticism by silence or by bringing out a true quality of the person being talked about.

Often we criticize because we are jealous or frustrated, as when we are waiting for others to consult us and they do not. It also happens that we project our own state of soul onto others. In criticism there is no love; the criticizer is left to himself, he obeys his evil tendencies. Criticism becomes a mania.

Miriam, the sister of Moses and Aaron, was particularly jealous of Moses who had married a Midianite woman. She was jealous of her brother because he received special favors from God who spoke to him regularly face to face. She imagined that she had the same rights as her brother but that through his egoism he put obstacles in her way.

Aaron, who was quite impressionable, was won over to her way of thinking. The situation became more serious; discontent and misunderstanding grew. Moses did not seem to be affected by the situation, therefore God himself defended his servant. The Lord intervened and censured their pride. Miriam was struck down with leprosy and it was only after seven days of intercession that Moses obtained the healing of his sister. Miriam understood; peace returned. (cf. Nm 12) Miriam had criticized because she was frustrated.

History has already judged Hitler as one of the most cruel dictators of modern times. He is described as a modest, shy, silent man, turned in on himself, morose, taciturn, sensitive and susceptible. In 1914, he joined the German army and became part of a regiment destined to fight in Flanders where he had a number of tours of duty. His personality was strongly marked by his military life in the trenches. In Flanders he received his first baptism of fire: he was wounded in the thigh, was momentarily blinded and was intoxicated by gas.

It was in Flanders that he first came into contact with the Jews. It is said that his furious and irrational hatred for the Jews could have originated from a banal, seemingly unimportant incident. Hitler had a certain admiration for Hugo Gutmann, a Jewish ordinance officer, who obtained for him an important military citation: the Iron Cross, First Class. Corporal Hitler received this citation for his courage. Grateful to the officer, he accepted to deliver a package to a Jewish family in Nuremberg while he was on a week's leave there. But the officer's family did not welcome him properly; they made him wait; they answered him with indifference, they accepted the package distractedly and, to fill his cup to overflowing, they gave him a miserly tip of one mark for his troubles. Hitler passed through various interior states: he was literally torn apart, humiliated. He was no longer capable of finding any positive qualities in Jewish people and twenty years later when he became the head of his country, he sacrificed thousands of Jews in the crematory ovens. Hitler, frustrated, became inhuman. (*History for All*, no. 193)

When we allow criticism to take over, we no longer bear witness to God but to our frustrations. We must put as much care into concentrating on the presence of God as a technician in a laboratory places on his test-tubes. The life of someone may depend on it.

If we take on the compulsion of criticizing, others will not be duped, they will not believe in the vigor of our witness. They will say: "How did you get caught up in this affair? Is that what it means to be a Christian?" Gandhi used to say: "*I admire Christ*,

I love him, but I have no confidence in Christians." He judged by those he had seen in England in the course of his university studies.

Everyone knows that the *presence of God*, protected by an *absence of criticism*, is the basic element of the spiritual life and that the absence of criticism is a strong expression of Christian asceticism. All expect us to take on our responsibilities. Without a serious commitment to think of God, to be grafted onto him, to listen to his word and put it into practice, Christianity becomes a kind of social club which has no effect on our lives; it is incapable of leading us out of boredom or tepidity.

Those who speak well of others are seen as warm-hearted people who have common sense. If we recognize that we have joy, kindness, goodness, tenderness, gentleness and agreeableness in our hearts, we will not allow ourselves to become discouraged neither by evil nor by the aberrations or rigorous judgements of others. We will find enough indulgence in our hearts not to blast out condemnations. We will be able to distinguish between the evil to be rejected, and the authors of evil who need our mercy and our friendship.

Goodness is surely the most visible manifestation of the presence of God. The day we are no longer tempted to judge others unfavorably or harshly, our relationships with them will become marvelous. The *absence of criticism* fortifies the presence of God, educates us to patience, augments the spiritual forces within us, permits us to welcome our neighbor with simplicity, stimulates our heart, weans our imagination, pacifies our passions, calms emotivity, suffocates our instincts for revenge, liberates us from selfishness and pettiness, and preserves intimacy with God.

When we let ourselves go and criticize destructively, we become our own worst enemy. We neglect the Lord, withdraw into ourselves, manifest a certain disrespect for others and become the plaything of our passions. We deliver ourselves into the hands of our evil tendencies and lose control of our emotivity. Being that love is ignored, it no longer directs our attitudes and our sentiments.

To criticize is to affirm a certain superiority over others, to give ourselves a diploma of competence, to assume, perhaps unconsciously, the place of God. To judge is an attribute belonging to God and not to us. Let us learn not to meddle in the affairs of others. Let us have confidence in God and not be afraid for he has a solution to every problem; in every discussion the last word belongs to him. By judging we do not facilitate his task; we only hurt ourselves and others.

To speak of the *presence of God* is to speak of intimacy with God. We can easily think of God, say beautiful things about him yet still be far from him, far from his will. We find many such examples in the Gospels. The first person to announce to the people that Jesus was the Messiah, the son of God, was one possessed by a devil. (cf. Mk 1:23-24)

St. Mark's Gospel speaks of certain Pharisees, criticizers, who want to find fault with Jesus. The Pharisees detest him, they speak of him every time his name comes to mind. A small group of them get together, criticize him, elaborate plans, and set traps to catch him in an error. Without realizing it they are being illogical and stupid. They send a group of colleagues to speak with Jesus. It is a setup. The delegates ask a question but first of all they prepare the ground. Able in psychology, endowed with good intelligence, they have picked out the good qualities in Jesus. Thus they say to him: "*Master, we know you are a truthful man and that you are not concerned with anyone's opinion. You do not regard a person's status but teach the way of God in accordance with the truth."*

All these affirmations are true, yet even though they are standing close to Jesus they are not in his presence because they do not have faith in him. They hate him, dispute him and desire his death. Malice and hatred have sealed their hearts, and their knowledge of him serves only to hide their cunning and their bad faith. They ask a question: *"Is it lawful to pay the census tax to Caesar or not?"* If Jesus says yes, we must pay the tax, we are under the authority of the Romans, then the Pharisees will denounce him to the Israelites as a renegade who has delivered himself to the Romans, the colonizers of the country. This first affirmation will have all the Israelites on his back. If, on the other hand, Jesus says no, do not pay, the cost of living is very high, Caesar always has too much money to oppress us then the Pharisees will hasten to denounce him as a zealot, an anarchist, a separatist and the Romans will deal harshly with him. They are happy with their well-thought-out plan. They are certain of the efficacy of their trap. They are already rubbing their hands together in triumph. They believe that they have foreseen everything.

Jesus probes hearts and minds; he unmasks their slyness and hypocrisy. He responds with a question that appears inoffensive and harmless: *"Bring me a denarius to look at.... Whose image and inscription is this?"* They replied to him: *"Caesar's."* *"Repay to Caesar what belongs to Caesar and to God what belongs to God."* They were utterly amazed at him. They went away not daring to make another attempt. (cf. Mk 12:13-17)

In order for the presence of God to be transforming it must mobilize our hearts. When we accept the Lord he comes to dwell in us; he is as much at home in our hearts as he was when he went to the house of Lazarus and of Zaccheus. All our faculties are tuned in to Jesus ready to put themselves at his service. Under this affectionate awareness, our whole being feels itself transformed and transfigured. God is certain that, like Mary Magdalene, we too will understand the language of love.

2. The Damaging Effects of Criticism

Why not take the time to consider some of the damaging effects of destructive criticism? We must reflect at length on this subject because very few people strive to combat criticism, even though everyone knows the damage it causes. It is difficult to believe that we ourselves are effected by this scourge. We have the impression that this subject is useful only for others. Obviously, we admit that at times we may accidentally fall into criticism. Still, everyone does it so we tell ourselves that we are not worse than others and put our conscience to rest.

Let us ask the Holy Spirit to revive our intelligence, our wisdom, our knowledge, our counsel, our piety, our strength, our fear of the Lord so that we may work for our own spiritual evolution.

I point out here numerous damaging effects of *destructive criticism.* The list is necessarily incomplete; you can add your own personal experiences to it. Destructive criticism can turn an easy duty into a difficult task. It stops us from discovering positive values in ourselves and in others. It causes us to become disgusted with certain people that we could help. It weakens or destroys courage. It renders us vulnerable, excites our passions, smothers the voice of remorse. It causes the loss of self-control and makes us more emotional, aggressive, morose, less pious, drawing us away from prayer. It slows down the positive evolution of our personality and upsets or disturbs our degree of concentration. It makes us an easier prey to mental or moral fatigue and blocks simplicity in our relationship with God. It diminishes or destroys our inclination and attraction to place ourselves in the presence of God. It renders the criticizer contemptible in the eyes of those who listen. Friends become nervous wondering if they'll be the next victims. The criticizer never bothers to ask pardon and is surprised by the reaction of his victims.

Holy Scripture uses stronger tones than we would dare to use in describing the damage caused by the tongue. It often uses a direct and picturesque style such as St. James does in chapter 3 verses 2-13 of his letter.

"With it [the tongue] we bless the Lord and Father, and with it we curse human beings who are made in the likeness of God." (Jas 3:9)

"From the perverse tongue flows forth lies, guile, duplicity, scandal, calumny." (Ps 10:7) "The tongue is a serpent." (Ps 140:4) "It is a sharpened razor." (Ps 52:4) "It is a sharp sword." (Ps 57:5) "It is a murderous arrow." (Jer 9:7)

Destructive criticism often monopolizes the spirit, overexcites the nerves, causes anxiety, and creates tensions that become difficult to bear.

Criticism originates in self-love. It can be personified as a devil who stands at the door of the heart sowing trouble, changing the current of our positive thoughts and throwing confusion into our imagination which has a marked tendency for exaggeration and dramatization. When the devil does not succeed in introducing himself into the heart of a person, he disturbs them, he takes away their joy and peace and they become so anemic that the presence of God no longer interests them.

There is an incompatibility of nature between the presence of God and destructive criticism. They cannot live under the same roof: when one is present the other disappears. They are like light and darkness. As the light approaches, darkness moves away. As destructive criticism approaches, the presence of God leaves.

We must be conscious enough to accept these realities not as an interesting theory but as a way of life. If we criticize, we so weaken our presence of God that it is incapable of stimulating our capacity to love and to be transformed. The habit of criticizing does not take away our spiritual language but it destroys fervor, the taste for perfection and the desire for intimate union with God.

Let us learn to aim at the essential. In a relationship the essential is always sensitivity, comprehension, a gift of self to the person who is near us. Let us ignore matters of little importance, not wasting time with accidentals, details, appearances, compulsions, with little irritating defects. Let us look beyond the misadventures that happen along the way. Let us endeavor to go right to the heart of God and our neighbors to reach the richness of their being.

If we were able to grasp all the disastrous subtleties of destructive criticism, all the damage produced both in the criticizer and in the victim — often a person who is absent and does not have the chance to beg for mercy — we would change our behavior and strive wholeheartedly to live an affectionate presence of God.

Let us examine ourselves seriously, it is possible that we have more than just a simple tendency to criticize. Perhaps we say things that are disagreeable and harmful. We may not yet have an uncontrollable habit, but if we are often taciturn, morose, and dejected, if our attitude expresses pessimism and our face always appears to be frowning at people or events, we should ask ourselves: Are we in harmony with God who asks us to have a preferential love for him and an unconditional love for others? Do we want to succeed in playing our part in the divine plan? Then let us keep an eye on destructive criticism and keep a strict control over it.

Monsignor Charles Eugene Mathieu was secretary general of the Canadian Bishops for ten years. He was a special person gifted with the heart of an apostle and a communicative piety. For some years, through the creation of a movement called *Pax Vobis* (Peace be with you) he endeavored to establish a network of communications — radio and television — throughout Canada which would be uniquely Christian. During his lifetime he was often a helpless witness to bitter criticisms. He saw so many persons whose reputations were wounded and broken that he worked to be the herald of charity and peace. In the rules that laid out the good functioning of his organization, he wrote: "Each member, lay, religious or cleric, will work to carry out with discretion and tact, but above all by their own example, a daily, tenacious war against all that risks destroying, directly or indirectly, publicly or privately, the unity, credibility and good morale of the members of the Church and of the team *Pax Vobis*. Among other things, we will vigorously combat the least lack of fraternal charity, authoritative pronouncements, virtual excommunications, the all-too-easy accusations, the frequent gossiping, the negative rumors, and news that is uselessly depressing, the detestable, chronic denigration of all that others do elsewhere or in a different manner; all types of manipulation, intrigue, and sectarianism, whatever good intentions are involved."

The list is long, Monsignor wanted it to be complete and this proscription in favor of charity leaves no room for exceptions. Those who do not pay attention to it will be sent away from the team, whatever their rank, their dignity, their talents. Here is the price of charity, to get rid of criticism, no matter what form it takes.

Criticism is a wound that paralyzes associations. Those who give in to this excess, diminish their reputations in the sight of those who have listened. We are led to pity and sometimes to a repugnance for those who criticize.

We must not only avoid criticism but also fight energetically against certain formulas used by many people today. These formulas are the ingenuity of the devil and we naively borrow them because we do not have enough mettle to keep quiet. Here are formulas that we should banish without pity: I shouldn't tell you this but... I do not want to lack charity, but... I do not want to be indiscreet, but... I think that it is my duty to tell you... I admit that this person has good qualities, but...

Why not react generously against these phrases which bear a diabolical subtlety. We must consider the "but" as an invitation made to the devil to pour his poison into the conversation. Why not adopt the philosophy of the Alcoholics Anonymous? Why not attack this gangrene, this criticism, by promising for each 24 hours a sobriety in our words, meetings, conversations and our way of treating our neighbor. This promise must be renewed every 24 hours, keeping in mind that the Gospel affirms that each day has its own sufferings. The cross imposed by the absence of criticism is proportionate to what we can lift up and carry in a day. To protect ourselves, we might have to remain far from certain criticizers, avoiding them like we avoid smokers when we have a horror of smoking or of lung cancer.

3. Advantages of the Absence of Criticism

The objective of the presence of God is to keep us in our true place in God's plan. The absence of criticism helps us to preserve this place without difficulty. We often say that the term *absence of criticism* and the other term *absence of complaint* are too negative to be interesting. Do not judge too hastily: the realities contained in these terms are truly positive.

To gain a better understanding, let us personalize the term *absence of criticism*. Let us say that the term indicates a person; let's call this person our guardian angel, the watchman, the bodyguard of the presence of God. In effect, the *absence of criticism* is an angel that marches at our side to protect our relationship with God, like the angel who directed Moses. The *absence of criticism* is the bodyguard who is always present, never tired, who stands like a watchman to survey the presence of God so that it will be strong and avoid the attacks of criticism.

What happens within me when I am careful to avoid criticism? I sense that the call of the Lord is stronger, I recognize that the presence of God is easier to live on a deeper level. The Holy Spirit is closer, I can grasp him better with the eyes of my heart; my life with God is more serious. I have the supernatural intuition that the gifts of the Spirit, the charisms and fruits are not beyond me; I do not need to go looking for them. I sense that they are within me, living in me; that they are a part of my life, that they function and I consider them as blessings. The Holy Spirit lives in me like one who acts in complete liberty, without fear of breaking a friendship. I realize that I am made for him and he is all mine.

To carry on this experience of supernatural life, I must consider the absence of criticism as a sympathetic person, a friend, an angel who constantly stands guard over me so that I do not lose the deposit of faith. If the presence of God opens me to a climate of intimacy, if it floods my heart with the peace that no enjoyment or human value can give me, it is because the absence of criticism plays its part well and is careful to see that my relationship with God is undisturbed. The *absence of criticism* is a friend who keeps an eye on me in all my relationships with others so that charity will be safeguarded. This absence of criticism must, like an angel, live at my side, accompany me day and night and warn me of dangers. It must teach me the value of silence and discretion in my speech, the irresistible and contagious force of true love, and the powerful effects of mercy and pardon.

Why not consider the absence of criticism like the archangel Raphael who accompanied young Tobias to protect him against dangers, to send the evil spirits fleeing and to save him from certain death? He brought Tobias home with the power and means necessary for healing his elderly father and to discover in this voyage the presence of God and his will.

4. Unconditional Love of Our Neighbor

An excellent means for combatting destructive criticism is love of our neighbor. On many occasions, I have pointed out the way to combat criticism, which comes from tendencies that we do not sufficiently control. As St. Francis said: "*Where there is hatred, let me sow love.*"

Love, peace, joy and amiability are antidotes for criticism. Although it is true that the tongue can bring about pernicious effects, it is nonetheless true that it can be one of the greatest riches that we possess. The prophet Isaiah said that to give speech to the mute is a Messianic work: "*Say to those whose hearts are frightened: Be strong, fear not! Here is your God... he comes to save you. Then will the lame leap like a stag, then the tongue of the dumb will sing.*" (Is 35:4-6)

The well-trained tongue speaks marvels; it conveys the riches of the heart; it can lift our whole being to the summits of God's praises. The author of Proverbs affirms: "*The tongue of the just is like choice silver...*" (Prv 10:20) "*It recounts the justice of the Lord, it proclaims the praises of God.*" (Ps 35:27) It confesses the universal power of God; like our lips it makes known our heart.

All the same, we must always keep in mind the advice given by the apostles James and John and it is also useful to know the thoughts of King David, a man close to the heart of God, even though he had his hour of sin. James tells us: "*If anyone thinks he is religious and does not bridle his tongue, but deceives his heart, his religion is vain.*" (Jas 1:26) David a long time before had warned us: "*Keep your tongue from evil and your lips from speaking guile. Turn from evil and do good. Seek peace and follow after it.*" (Ps 34:14-15) He adds that in his conduct, he will guard his tongue from error: "*O God set a watch before my mouth, a guard at the door of my lips. Let not my heart incline to evil, of engaging in deeds of evil...*" (Ps 141:3-4)

St. John, the preacher of hope and love, tells us with his usual gentleness: "*Children, let us love not in word or speech but in deed and truth. ...if our hearts condemn us, God is greater than our hearts and knows everything. Beloved, if our hearts do not condemn us, we have confidence in God and receive from him whatever we ask...*" (1 Jn 3:18-22)

We will be able to block our evil tendencies if we develop the presence of God, if we keep watch over our tongue, if we endeavor to concretely love our neighbor. I want to insist on this love, this welcome, this warm relationship that we must have with our neighbor.

At times we can ask if it is a good thing to have a free will which permits us to make choices. We do not need to be faced with many choices or many alternatives to become hesitant, confused and awkward. Our approaches to our neighbor are varied, therefore it is dangerous to be satisfied with merely superficial contacts.

In fact there are three avenues that lead to our neighbor: our *feelings,* our *intelligence,* and the *profound richness of our being* which has at the same time exquisite feelings, a precious intuition and a warm heart.

a) *Feelings*

I *feel* drawn toward a certain category of people, I like meeting them, greeting them, smiling at them, showing a certain interest in them. What is it that draws me? Their physique, the beauty of their face, the regularity of their features, their distinguished way of acting, their way of dressing, their overall appearance: phlegmatic, calm, poised, stylish? Or perhaps their enthusiasm, their sensibility, their emotivity? In any case, whenever I see them I feel my heart open to welcome them; I sense that such a friendship could bring me much good.

Throughout our lives, we have rubbed elbows with hundreds of people whom we found sympathetic, who exercised a certain sensible attraction, an attraction that released in us a whole chain of emotions which upset us interiorly and gave us the impression that our senses had been turned upside down. This is one way of going to others, of welcoming them but it is not the best way because the criteria for these friendships is too fragile; we are too selective. Instead, we must go to everyone, welcome everyone. Feelings are like magnets that only stick to certain kinds of metal. This sensible attraction is too limited, it limits our capacity to love.

If this is the only avenue I use, I will find that whenever my feelings have been disappointed I will become hypersensitive, open to all kinds of destructive criticism.

b) *Intelligence*

I can go towards others on a second avenue: that of my *intelligence*. I can allow myself to be drawn by those who have titles, diplomas, a certain way of thinking, of explaining techniques and of presenting ideas and principles. I like their way of reasoning, their method of arguing, of writing a thesis, of demolishing another. When I am with these people I strive to reason; I, too, want to appear intelligent. I admire the culture of this one, the business sense of that one, their education, their humor, the solidity of their practical judgement.

Those on the first avenue caused me a bit of excitement. Those on the second avenue fill me with admiration and respect. If I limit my friendships simply to those on this second way I am still being too selective and each time I make a selection I reject from my friendship a crowd of interesting people.

These two avenues must open out onto a third avenue otherwise I will be superficial, hypersensitive, a neo-intellectual bound by the limits that my imagination has created. The first two routes are useful, we cannot avoid them but they lead to a dead end if we stop; they are good only when we use them to go forward.

c) *The Profound Richness of Our Being*

Nature can give us excellent examples. We can say that the third avenue is that of the bees. They leave their hive and travel for distances of up to forty kilometers in one journey. They fly over fields of forage or flowers; they land, draw out what is best in the flowers, go back to their hive, and work to produce the finest honey. The honey depends on the richness of the flower, the instinct of the bee and its work. The bee does not analyze the flower which shares a part of its riches with it, nor does it allow itself to be captured by its sensibilities. It knows that it must return to the hive, that its work is waiting and it wants to be faithful to its mission. The bee is concerned only about the quality of the flower.

There is a third route open to each human being for reaching others: the *profound richness of our being*. A richness made up of talents, gifts, aptitudes, energy, dynamism, various capacities such as the power to love, to understand, to use free will, to be capable of making choices, to create a climate of confidence in others and to assume responsibilities.

This combination of values constitutes our personality, that which comes forth from the hands of God at the hour of our birth and which was embellished by grace on the day that we became Christians. This avenue leads to others and helps us to discover the best that is in each of them; this helps to produce in us a quality of intimacy with God.

Intimacy with God is always proportional to the quality of the love we have for our neighbor. On this third avenue, there is no selecting, no restriction. It is not appearance that counts, not a brilliant intelligence that draws us but the whole person, the fullness of being, the complete image, the total child of God.

These three avenues coexist in every human being, but only one — the third — permits us to overcome destructive criticism because it enables us to accept others for the best that is in them: their richness of being. Our movement towards others must be unconditional and not be released by a simply sensible or intellectual attraction.

In fact, that is the route Jesus used in the course of his life on earth. Why did he call Matthew to be an apostle? Matthew, because of his trade, had the reputation of being dishonest. What sensible attraction could have drawn him to Zaccheus who was seen as petty and avaricious? Why this disconnected conversation on the cross with one who had been judged a bandit, was condemned and was going to die in twenty minutes? We only have one answer: the third avenue, the unconditional acceptance of the other. Jesus was more interested in the salvation of Mary Magdalene than by what could have been considered a flirt.

One of the most efficacious means of combatting destructive criticism is endeavoring to love our neighbor gratuitously.

5. The Disinterested Encounter with Others

a) *Love Our Enemies*

The Lord asks us to love our neighbor, even our enemies if we have any. This love is not based on gratitude or on the kindness of others, but on the words of Christ. Therefore, we must no longer build friendships by calculating what advantages others can bring us, what they can do for us. Our love must find its source in the capabilities of our own being. It must be stimulated by the word and example of Christ. Thus we will be able to emulate the 22nd president of the United States, William McKinley, who was shot to death by an anarchist and socialist worker, Leon F. Czolgosz. This worker wanted to kill the president simply because he did not accept his way of running the country.

On September 6, 1901, the President arrived at the Panamerican exposition of Buffalo, New York. That day, at the "Temple of Music," a reception was being given in his honor. He had a dozen body-guards all around him and eight others who minutely surveyed the situation. Eleven soldiers were inside the Temple, while three secret service agents and four police inspectors from Buffalo escorted him step by step; they did not leave his side for a second. Numerous visitors wanted to greet the President. They were placed in line and were inspected one by one. Leon F. Czolgosz got in line with the others, he pretended to be wounded and had a bandage on his arm, but his bandage hid the murder weapon, an Iver Johnson, 32-caliber pistol.

Smiling, President McKinley shook hands with each one. A little girl accompanied by her father drew the benevolence of the President. She was followed by a robust, tough-looking Italian, who drew the attention of the bodyguards; they hurried him on and let the young worker, who seemed to have a wounded hand, come forward. McKinley, saw the bandage, smiled, and went towards the young man, who suddenly shot twice. The President crumpled to earth; the guards overcame the assassin. A tall, black, athletic-looking man named Parker sought to grab the worker; he had a knife in his hand ready to kill him. McKinley, seeing his assassin lying on the ground under a barrage of kicks, painfully lifted his right hand, red with his own blood and in a feeble voice begged: "*Gently, my friends, gently.*" Then he turned toward his secretary and asked him to make sure that no harm be done to the worker.

McKinley died eight days later murmuring, "*If it were not for Ida, my spouse, I would have liked to go like Lincoln...*" That is what he did early the morning of September 13, 1901. McKinley had love in his heart even for his enemies because he believed in God. (*Mirror of History,* no. 283, p. 87)

The Lord tells us to love but he does not want us to demand a recompense. The good that we sow must be given freely. We must not expect to receive only good from others. This kind of love is profound and goes beyond the idea of capitalism; it is a way of reasoning that mocks natural philosophy.

It is the Gospel, it is Divine. We can love others with our senses allowing ourselves to be attracted by their physical qualities, their features, their affability or the suppleness of their gestures. We can love others and take the time to listen to them, to let them tell their story, to admire the limpidity of their thoughts, the logic of their reasoning, their sudden burst of brilliance, but we still have not gone far enough or deep enough. We must search carefully to discover what is in their hearts: their way of loving, of letting themselves be loved, their way of being honest, loyal, just, true, tender, comprehensive human beings. We must discover the profound riches of the other. The presence of God is nourished when we clarify the why of this deep attraction.

We will love others, if we put our hearts into serving them, into accepting our differences and avoiding animosity whatever their mood happens to be. We will love others if we listen to them and we strive to understand them, if we avoid monopolizing them, if we have confidence in them, if we discover positive qualities in them and have the courage to give them credit for these qualities; if we are happy when others seem to be exalted, acclaimed and congratulated. We will love others, even our enemies, if we do not allow the spirit of vengeance to infiltrate us and if we are able to pardon.

To love is a duty of the heart not of the senses or the mind. This duty is given us by the Lord; the presence of God makes it possible insofar as this presence is not weakened by destructive criticism.

59

When we avoid destructive criticism we dispose ourselves to love others profoundly and we can be sure that we do not extinguish the Spirit in us, that we do not sadden him.

b) *Let the Profound Love of Others Be Born in Us*

This love is neither a product of the intellect nor of the will. It does not originate from a series of resolutions we make to love. Nor does it come from the demands of a will resolved to overcome all difficulties and repugnances in order to carry out its duty to love in a suitable fashion. This profound love surges forth from the heart without effort. It is like the sap in a maple tree or a light produced by a little wick that allows itself to fall into the oil that will impregnate it. This love is obtained without violence, without exertion. We must simply endeavor to discover in ourselves the presence of a living, acting, loving God, who manifests himself each time we become aware of one or another positive qualities of our being.

If we were to set out to discover the positive in others, we would have the same impression as the sculptor who liberates from the strong trunk of a tree the image that dwells within himself. In order to find his work of art in a tree, the sculptor must first of all be aware that the work of art is within himself, in his own heart.

Profound love springs forth from our inner self, from the depths of our being, and takes on the form of those positive qualities which are most important and most agreeable. These qualities are in our depths, we have had them since birth. At our baptism they were enriched, ennobled, and reinforced sufficiently so that we could understand Jesus, his teachings, his examples, his way of loving. As Isaiah states: *"If you would harken to my commandments, your happiness would be like a river, and your integrity like the waves of the sea..."* (Is 48:18) The whole being is irrigated with peace, silent joy and stabilizing serenity. This deep love orients and stimulates the energies within us, liberating them from all danger of aggressivity, of contestation, of disputes and criticisms. This love is at the service of all the positive that we can easily detect in our neighbor.

We do not seek to avoid criticism through wise reasonings or harsh resolutions, but by focusing our energies on discovering the qualities of others. These qualities become a nourishment that pleases love which needs substance in order not to become anemic.

c) *Let the Love of Others Grow in Us*

Love was meant to grow; whatever the path we are walking, progress is always possible. Perhaps we are on the threshold of a depression, on the point of breaking off a friendship or ready to leave our team. No matter; nothing is lost; it is never too late. We must examine our love. Have we perhaps ceased gathering the positive? Do we put a brake on our imagination when it spouts out destructive criticism? We must adjust our love and start over again every 24 hours. This is the normal task of a Christian; thus we will merit our salary.

Starting over again signifies:

— that we return to our search for the positive in others, especially in those who upset us. We will try to overcome feelings, and susceptibilities in order to detect the riches in the hearts of others. To make a meditation is not a waste of time, it is in fact a form of prayer agreeable to the Lord. *"Therefore, if you bring your gift to the altar and there recall that your brother has anything against you, leave your gift there at the altar, go first and be reconciled with your brother..."* (Mt 5:23-24)

— that we do not allow ourselves to be overcome by negativity. Our neighbor seems to be hateful, his conduct inconceivable, his unkindness and lack of consideration are unexplainable. We must not hold on to such reasonings otherwise we will poison our own existence and may harm the person we are speaking to for years to come. We must willingly look for the positive in the other. If necessary, we will consult his best friends to find these positive qualities.

Only the positive suscitates wonder. Wonder is the solid platform of profound love. Profound love presupposes that our self-forgetfulness is strong enough to bring about sincere pardon, which touches the heart and even the memory. It is here that Christians give themselves fully and become witnesses to Christ. They become facsimiles of

Christ that even the blind are able to read. We must run away from negative or destructive criticism realizing that it can empty us of profound love. Normally, when we find ourselves caught up in conversations that describe the misdeeds or faults of others, we should withdraw quietly. Criticizers wound themselves each time they succumb to their habit of demolishing others.

d) *Protect Our Way of Loving Others*

It is necessary for us to protect ourselves by:

— fighting our lack of personal depth. We must avoid living uniquely on the feeling level of our being. We are easily startled; disagreeable judgements can pile up to our detriment and to the detriment of our neighbor. We must not allow ourselves to be guided only by our instincts, by an unhealthy sensitivity or a susceptibility that is always on edge.

— avoiding to meet others only on the intellectual level, otherwise we provoke endless discussions that cause hearts to shrivel up and die.

— exercising the practice of the presence of God often throughout the day. Thinking of the damage caused by destructive criticism, of the richness of the Lord who is the rightful proprietor of all those whom he made in his own image and likeness. Our neighbors give us the chance to discover in them this image of God; why let our

search be aborted because of a few idle or negative words?

If we want to learn to love in depth, we must
free ourselves from an overemotional sensitivity in
order to consider the riches deposited in us by our
Creator. We should think of the enthusiasm that
the search for the positive creates in each of us. It
is a marvelous way of seeking God. The psalmist
says: "... *those who seek the Lord want for no good
thing.*" (Ps 34:11)

If we want our love to become more profound
we must take the time to deepen it. If one day
someone says to me: "This year I have sought daily
to find all the positive qualities in myself and in
others; at times, I gave others credit for the results
of my discoveries. I have had no other form of
prayer, except the frequentation of the sacraments,
an ordinary liturgical life and the daily recitation of
some psalms," I would congratulate them because
their instinct for criticism would be completely
weakened and their presence of God would be
strong and healthy. As Jesus used a wild flower to
lead his apostles to the presence of his Father, so
the one who seeks the positive will find qualities
that will lead him right to the Father.

Let's not be afraid to take time to discover
positive qualities in other members of your team,
in your work milieu, in your social milieu, in your
family, in the hierarchy of the Church, in our
institute, in our community.

Let's take time, either individually or with others, to create favorable occasions for discovering

what is positive. This is how we will regain a sense of wonder, an optimistic joy, a durable light-heartedness and a contagious dynamism. Then our faces too, like those of the apostles on Pentecost morning, will reflect Christ.

May Mary Immaculate help us to revise our personal lives, anesthetize our natural tendencies to destructive criticism, reinvigorate our ardor for discovering the qualities of others and live the presence of the Trinity. Our five attitudes of soul create in us a way of thinking and acting in conformity with the Holy Spirit. This is marvelous for opening us to the riches of the Church: the sacraments, the liturgy, apostolic action, the sense of Scriptures and a love for prayer.

If every Christian would accept to live these five attitudes each 24 hours, the world would become a furnace of warmth for the heart of Jesus, a warmth that attracts and comforts others.

Absence of Complaint

If we look superficially at the term "absence of complaint," it seems negative. It might not carry much weight for the committed Christian, especially for one who is consecrated, who officially before the Church, has promised to tend toward perfection.

Let us note that this apparently negative manner of speaking presupposes an awareness of our relationship with God and a love for our neighbor. Let us recognize that this attitude toward complaint permits us to acquire self-control and channels our energies enabling us to accept our profession and our work milieu. It would be unwise to ignore this means of perfection of humanity.

Let us not be stopped by these words: "absence of complaint." Let us seek to find in this seemingly sad facade all the perfection contained within, all the efforts that it may require.

Absence of complaint is not easy to live. We must be constantly on guard; if we relax our attention for a moment we can be dragged along in a torrent of moaning and groaning. Without realizing it, we become weaker and our sense of wonder is lessened.

1. Terminology

If we think seriously about the *absence of complaint*, we realize that it is a gift of God that cannot be separated from the sense of wonder. Those who persist in complaining about events and things around them can be considered like blind people who are incapable of discovering around them those little positive aspects which give birth to enthusiasm and create an open spirit filled by optimism.

On the contrary, if we endeavor to avoid complaint, we will feel a sense of wonder surge up from our souls, a wonder which has the power to radiate light on everything, a brilliant light full of human warmth. We will discover in ourselves an artist's heart ready to embellish all that surrounds us. All nature, work, dedication and generosity, as well as all events will develop an incredible creativity in us. We will be sowers of light and life.

Those who avoid complaint feel the need to go beyond themselves, to gather the positive everywhere: in everyday life, in nature, in what they see, in the events that they must accept. They sharpen all their senses in order to capture the beautiful, the good, the positive and the true, to create in themselves a vast openness so that their interior heaven may be inhabited by universal beauty.

The *absence of complaint* is a guilelessness that the Lord places in our eye; it helps us to unearth all that is positive, useful and agreeable in our work, in our service, in events. "*If your eye is sound, your whole body will be filled with light.*" (Mt 6:22; Lk 11:34)

The *absence of complaint* is truly a strength that comes from God. By ourselves, we are unable to be quiet or to speak at the right moment. At the moment when the disciples rejected the project of the Eucharist, Peter responded to Jesus' question both in his name and in the name of his companions. Jesus said to him: "*Blessed are you Simon, son of Jonah. For flesh and blood has not revealed this to you but our heavenly Father.*" (Mt 16:17) A few moments later Jesus spoke of his coming death and Peter opposed such a subject of conversation that could disturb the peace of the group. Jesus rebuked Peter and said to him: "*Get behind me Satan, you are an obstacle to me. You are thinking not as God does but as human beings do.*" (Mt 16:23; Mk 8:33) Like Peter we are open to the Spirit but unfortunately we can also unconsciously become the plaything of the devil.

The *absence of complaint* is a way of disconnecting ourselves from evil tendencies and of referring all to God, without whom we can do nothing. It is God who through his Spirit gives us the strength and the energy to accept a work or a trade and who gives us the light necessary to bring out all that is useful in events which may appear negative at first sight.

The *absence of complaint* helps us to discern God's way of governing the world, his way of directing each of us, of using events to mold us, orient us and motivate our reactions. He places an attraction for perfection within us; he gives us energy, courage, and dynamism, so that we can attain results.

The *absence of complaint* protects the sense of wonder in each of us. It gives us the desire to scrutinize events and to discover in them the divine will. It opens our minds and hearts to all that is positive in creation. It's objective is to help us concentrate on those qualities which give us a finishing touch and a visible perfection. It assures discipline, favors education and reinforces our Christian witness. It keeps our heart serene, our face joyful and our whole being in simplicity and spontaneity.

The *absence of complaint* moderates our attraction to sensible pleasure; it encloses our being within the limits of honesty; it mortifies, purifies, tempers, and masters our sensitivity. It revitalizes us and gives us an aspect of humility that renders us more welcoming and sociable.

The *absence of complaint* gives deep serenity to those who serve. Service offered in a complaining and grumbling spirit may be accepted because of necessity but it closes hearts and creates a persistent shyness. Service given with a smile and a willing heart is often the beginning of a durable friendship.

The *absence of complaint* vitalizes, and helps us to generously accept a difficult mission or a painful duty. It helps us to concentrate more fervently on what we are asked to do.

The exterior *absence of complaint* implies a free heart, because wonder is something that gushes forth from the heart and its number one enemy is complaint.

The *absence of complaint* manifests the spiritual maturity of a person, it expresses the basic quality of a personality which tends toward self-control.

The *absence of complaint* indicates a beautiful personality, one who has taken charge of his life, who has a sense of responsibility, who bears witness to vital dynamism and contagious energy. We sense the action of the Holy Spirit in this person who avoids complaint by developing patience, fidelity, perseverance, and self-control.

The *absence of complaint* demands that each of us make a constant effort which we call asceticism. The habit of avoiding complaint favors a spirituality which invites us to live in the light of the Lord and to benefit from his warm, paternal presence.

As we personified the absence of criticism, we can also give a face to the absence of complaint. Let us say that it is a delicate, discreet angel whom the Lord places at our side, to remind us that we are people of service, an impossibility if we live in the midst of complaint. Complaint is repulsed by service. The *absence of complaint* is an angel of peace who invites each of us to express all the positive elements that we can extract from our work, from our profession, from the events we have lived. This angel draws our attention to our quality of service rather than to our deficiencies. It shows us the advantages of our trade, of our employment and helps us to love all the instruments that we use to serve.

The mission of *absence of complaint* is to quiet the imagination and to sensitize the heart to the beauties of life. It is the bodyguard of the sense of wonder, the watchman who stands guard over the whole person to keep him in a state of service.

Perhaps we know where we are going and we know the roads that lead there, but in moments of confusion who can brag that they do not need a guide? We know that God is our most effective point of reference; the absence of criticism protects the presence of God. The absence of complaint plays an analogous role, keeping us fixed in the love of our duty of state, activating our aspirations to dedication, animating our capacities to serve, accelerating our availability.

2. Definition of Complaint

Let's look around us, let's notice the people who strive not to criticize or complain; their faces are relaxed, they are friendly, welcoming, often they have a sense of humor. If we meet such people let us consider them the precious jewels that the Gospel speaks of and let us enter into a friendship with them. They will help us thanks to their maturity and self-control. At times we meet people who seem to adapt themselves to everything: they accept the sun or the rain, the summer or the winter with the same smile. With a bit of effort we can be like them; we have the same possibilities. It is simply a matter of considering our courage and setting to work.

On the other hand, we also come face to face with people who are always sad; they always have something to complain about. They have no control over their emotions. We sense that they are bitter, discontented, peevish and rebellious. Their faces are taunt and strained; their nerves are always on edge. Any little thing exasperates and irritates them. They continually think that others are picking on them, that they are being persecuted and they pose as victims. They are unhappy and far too much at the mercy of frustration; they cultivate anxiety, anguish, suspicion. The exterior complaint is a reflection of an embittered heart.

Let us try to give some descriptive definition of complaint and its damages. Then we will better understand the commandments of God that oblige us to love our neighbor and to seek the positive in his works.

Complaint is the exterior manifestation of discontentment in regard to something that touches us closely. It is the exteriorization of a frustrated sentiment; it is an unfavorable judgement made in regard to an object or an event either through weakness or through a lack of self-control. It is a depressing, pessimistic, negative expression of an uncontrolled sentiment.

Complaint and *criticism* are two contagious plagues of society; they are like air and noise pollution: only a few specialists try to do something about them. The majority of people are gradually poisoned in a more or less unconscious way.

Complaint is also a moaning, a murmuring provoked by a frustration or some contradiction. It is an act of impatience; our sensibilities become irritated, we become unbalanced by nervousness. *Complaint* is a cancer which ravages our sensibilities and

73

our countenance. It makes us gloomy; it dulls our smiles and diminishes the ardor of our heart. It stifles our energy, weakens our dynamism, shrivels us up and isolates us from others. It is a cancer that disfigures things and events, one which ruins our sense of wonder.

At first a *complaint* is only an idle word, a kind of "primo primi," a thoughtless reaction but then we sense that it is the product of immaturity, the invasion of our superior faculties (intelligence, will, conscience, heart) by foolish imaginings, unbridled sentiments and superficial or infantile manias.

Could the complainer be someone who has become handicapped: no longer supple, no longer having the ability to discover the plan of God in objects, events, nature or creation? Could they be persons who have become disabled: no longer capable of gazing in wonder at all that is beautiful? Could the complainer be those who are incompetent in their own eyes, who as time goes on see themselves as unloved, misunderstood, or victims? One would believe so, if these persons find it painful to take the blame, to modify their behavior or to overcome certain painful childhood experiences which left their mark. If they lose their self-confidence, if they prefer to complain rather than to react, if they prefer to remain in a cocoon rather than become a butterfly.

Complainers harass those who hear them; they disturb many people. Their presence is cumbersome; they love to call attention to themselves and to their suffering; they do not wish to be healed. Their conversations are as invariable as records never playing anything new. They always give out the same lamentations, the same demands and arguments.

Complaint causes considerable damage. Look at them, we will discover them on the periphery of our being. They set our nerves on edge; they are like a bad case of shingles, continually itching. Is it not better to make our own inventory of the damage? We will not have the courage to let another do it because we would soon feel demolished. Some of the harmful effects caused by complaint are: a lamenting or murmuring that diminishes the efficacy of our service to others; a cause for drawing together those caught up in the same weakness; a type of paralysis that takes the ardor out of our work and causes us to withdraw into ourselves and become depressed, insecure, weak. Nerves are ruined and we are driven into a multitude of personal problems.

Complaint lessens the gift of our will to God, changes love into doubt and suspicion, breaks the rhythm of generosity, cools our devotion and smothers spontaneity. It turns us away from others causing us to withdraw into ourselves. It makes us detest discipline and exaggerate suffering; it multiplies complexes, limits the impulses of our heart and renders hateful what should be attainable work.

3. How Can We Avoid Complaint?

It is unnecessary to mention that *complaint* does not depend on events, objects or the nature that surrounds us. All events and all objects in nature have two facets: one positive and one negative. If our judgement is more often negative, it is because something in us is not running smoothly. We will not find a solution or remedy outside of ourselves for our habit of complaining. It is within our own mind, heart and feelings that we must seek to rectify whatever is not functioning. We must come out of our torpor or our reveries, take ourselves in hand and concentrate on decisive daily efforts. We must bind ourselves to an asceticism and accept a certain discipline. Experience proves that it takes a lot of courage to eliminate the habit of complaining.

The beginnings of this personal asceticism are painful: we are afraid of ourselves and of others. We dread being taken for naive, old-fashioned, or a holier-than-thou. We are alarmed at the thought of being judged unfavorably if we go against the pressures of a society that has made criticizing and complaining a normal habit. In certain milieu, if we are not against something or someone, if we do not fight or make demands, it is taken as a sign that we lack leadership and personality. It takes courage to go against the current, to walk against the wind, to climb a steep slope.

If we succumb easily to our tendency to complain, we must recognize our faults, assume our own responsibilities and seriously question ourselves. We must get rid of this mania for seeing only the negative side of groups, communities, Institutes, associations; of seeing all their faults, defects and imaginable failures and of announcing our depressing discoveries to everyone. No one can correct themselves in the place of the other; it is a strictly personal affair.

We must all take charge of ourselves without worrying about what others will say. The development of our own personality demands it; true friends require it and in the Gospel Jesus himself begs us to become saints, taking the example of our heavenly Father. He commands us to love others, even those whom we perceive as enemies, adversaries, rivals or competitors. He points out the difference that must exist between a Christian, who is his disciple, and pagans. Pagans love those who love them and greet those who greet them. They love out of personal interest, for convenience or diplomacy; their love goes no further. But Christians must go beyond such reasoning. We must have respect for others and show them marks of friendship because this is what our heavenly Father asks of us, because the Lord himself wants to raise us to the heights of perfection.

In order to attain this exigent objective, we must even pray for our enemies, get rid of all rancor and free our minds from bad memories. We must forgive those who persecute us, who insult us, who lie about us. This is the prerequisite that enables the heart to take flight towards the heights of perfection. (cf. Mt 5:43-48) If we detest someone, he will easily become the target of our criticism. We will find fault with all that he does and will not hesitate to complain about it.

Avoiding complaint is possible if we impose a rigid discipline on ourselves, for example, knowing when to be silent or asking pardon of those present. We must learn to take our share of the blame, to ask forgiveness, to manifest regret, to focus our energies on making a new beginning. We must also know how to forget past complaints, to clean up our hearts so that they will be free. Past complaints contaminate our hearts just as much as present complaints do if we keep them within us as psychological fatigue or rancor. The badly-educated children of resentment are sulkiness, irritability, anguish and fear. We must tear them out of our hearts, our memories and our minds if we would eliminate criticism and complaint. We must begin again each new day, exerting ourselves to follow a known, accepted and lived discipline. To avoid complaint is to protect our mechanism of service to others and to live in the presence of God.

In an association, group, team or community, before all else we must accept this principle: a Christian must avoid destructive criticism and complaint. Once this principle has been recognized by individuals and by the collectivity, we will be less likely to be afraid, to pass for one who is expendable if we endeavor to avoid criticism and complaint. We may be tolerant toward those who have not yet become aware of this impediment to fraternal love but there is no reason to walk around as if we had the weight of the world on our shoulders simply because we are striving to overcome complaint.

When tepidity enters a group, people become afraid to speak of God; no one dares speak of graces received, or to carry a rosary. But those who bring this atmosphere into a group are not afraid to judge, condemn, criticize, complain, revindicate, or attack structures. Without realizing it, they have lost sight of their Christianity and taken on the traits of Marxism where contestation is an essential element of progress. Too often human respect, which in reality is only a lack of divine respect, causes us to do foolish things. We should be ashamed of our slackness, of our lack of ardor.

Let's make an effort in our milieu, so that the absence of complaint becomes a principle acceptable to everyone. Otherwise we will be obliged to excuse and defend ourselves for living attitudes demanded by our Christianity.

We must be personally convinced that to fight against criticism and complaint is a duty which it is not prudent to ignore or to treat lightly. If we do not have this conviction, it will become excessively difficult for us when we are in the midst of others who do not have the same ideals. Then tepidity, that distaste for effort, will reign in the group. The Holy Spirit will no longer have any influence because we will neither seek his presence nor his assistance.

Avoiding complaint constitutes a beneficial asceticism, helps to establish a solid relationship with God and fans into life the action of the Holy Spirit within us, an action that we are unable to stifle or extinguish. It is not easy to avoid complaint: we need willpower and we need to set our backs to the task, to stick to a daily regime. We must begin each day with the same ardor. It is not something we acquire once and for all. It is not a diploma that opens the door to the world of business. Rather it is a beast to dominate and a steed to bridle as St. James tells us. To conquer oneself supposes repeated, multiple efforts every 24 hours, otherwise we lose our concentration and we become dilettantes who lazily wait for good luck or a lottery prize to come their way in order to arrive at success. If the absence of criticism favors deepening our presence of God, the absence of complaint favors the quality of our service to others.

4. How Can We Fight Complaint?

We must struggle against *complaint* in order to become collectors of the positive, so that we may scrutinize objects, events, nature and creation with the eyes of the heart. This search for the positive keeps the heart young, it keeps away wrinkles. Isn't it better to pass for naive or even a bit simpleminded but conserve the right to cultivate expressions of wonder. This reputation will make us happier than the reputation of being a hard-hearted person who has something negative to say about everything, who brings sadness and a gloomy atmosphere with them wherever they go; whose mouth is twisted by criticism and complaint. The heart is a field in which the Holy Spirit has been sowing since our baptism. Are not criticism and complaint the weeds sown by the evil one to smother the good grain?

We must fight *complaint* if we want to develop an aptitude for detecting positive values in others. With a bit of good-natured observation, we will be able to congratulate others for their way of dressing, for their style, for their distinction, for the quality of their language. We will reveal the positive aspects of their intelligence and will. We will stop discrediting their style of thinking or their way of reasoning. If time and circumstances permit, we will have the joy of discovering profound qualities in those around us, such as their respect for others, their capacity for trusting, their sense of responsibility, their leadership, their qualities of courage, generosity, gentleness, and tenderness.

This is a marvelous and passionate study. We will have particularly stirring moments when, with simplicity, we reveal to others the results of our discoveries. We can already see them smiling as we tell them of the qualities we have discovered in them. Some will be sceptical while others will be stimulated and will thank God but all will be content. In these intense moments, we are truly living an outpouring of Christianity.

Let us not be stopped by old cliches disguised as proverbs, such as "compliments are often liars." They can be liars when they come only from the head but they are never false when they flow forth from the heart. The compliment that describes a positive attitude is contagious. When we receive it we are happy to repeat it to a friend in order to receive approval. It gives such pleasure to hear others speak well of us and our activities. We spring towards the Lord with more energy and run towards others to bring them a bit of sunshine.

How can we fight complaint? This is a question that we pose often enough but do we really take the time to allow a valid response to flow from our hearts? Often we ask ourselves questions but we rarely bother to take the time to seek answers within ourselves. These responses may be inconvenient because they require the use of energy, cause disturbances and change our habits.

Why work so hard to fight complaint? Because this is an essential element of the spiritual life to which the Christian must submit in order to live properly the first two commandments: love God above all else, love your neighbor as yourself.

By avoiding complaint, we reawaken in ourselves that sense of wonder which permits us to discover the positive aspects in others and in their work, positive aspects that become like well-lighted trails pointing out the way that leads to God.

It helps us to rediscover the sense of wonder which causes a reaction of astonishment/surprise to rise up in us when we see something agreeable and unexpected. Wonder is the spontaneous expression of a free and joyful heart. It is the infant's sudden awareness of the newness around him which leads him to the source of optimism. It is a vital dynamism that surges from the depths of our being, the serene energy that liberates, helps us to breathe and gives us the pleasure of creating.

5. Objective of the Absence of Complaint: Welcoming Events

We do not like to speak of complaint; we feel too vulnerable. As soon as the word is mentioned we are led to question ourselves. If we speak of absence of complaint we feel guilty; we know that perfection is not easy to attain. If the word "*complaint*" tires us, we can substitute another word such as: temperance. Instead of saying let's avoid complaint, we could say: be temperate, but we must admit that this terminology is more abstract, more general; it doesn't touch us so deeply.

What is more concrete, to say "be temperate" or "avoid complaint"? The two terms have the same objective, but the invitation is not as strong in both cases. To avoid *complaint* is a concrete expression that we can carry out more easily. It requires a direct effort; it calls us into question and gives the impression that when looking at ourselves in a mirror we make a more significant gesture by putting our finger to our lips to remind ourselves to be quiet.

We can manage to live without complaining if we strive to discover the lessons that we can learn from *events,* be they happy or unhappy. We must detect in them the positive meaning that can help us. Just as God speaks through the Bible, so also he speaks through events. We must listen if we want to grasp his message and receive it.

An *event* is a happy or unhappy fact that places us in sometimes unforeseen situations. It is a fact that assumes a certain importance, an invitation to become implicated in a new situation.

As we said, this event can be happy or unhappy. A happy event could be a promotion, the arrival of someone who betters my situation, a change that has been desired for a long time, a retreat, a meeting with a holy person, adherence to a resource group, etc.; perhaps it is something agreeable that was unexpected and surprising.

An event can also be unhappy. There are tragic, dramatic events which fall on us like calamities or catastrophes: a fire destroys our life savings; a company falls into bankruptcy; a person receives a change of obedience without warning; there is a psychological rejection from a person we love; a reputation is ruined by calumnies or false reports. An unexpected death, distressing news or a serious illness changes our best thought-out plans. An event never leaves us indifferent; it changes the present for better or for worse. Facing an event brings about three frequent attitudes; only one of them is profitable.

The *first attitude* is denial. We don't want to have anything to do with the event; we withdraw into our pain and accuse the Lord of being unjust. "Why do such things happen only to me." We persist in not submitting and even go so far as to abandon our religious practices. We break off all relations with God, proclaiming that prayer has no efficacy. We pray but nothing changes. In the depths of our hearts we nurture rancor, aggressivity and bitterness which causes others to say that we are rebellious.

The *second attitude* we can display when faced with an unhappy event is closing our heart. We hide the pain within ourselves while outwardly reacting as if we were above trials. We seek to distract ourselves; we refuse to speak of the problem and avoid those who would help us. Besides, as far as we're concerned they don't understand anything. We don't want them to speak about this hard blow which we are unable to accept. Interiorly, we become intoxicated; we are hedged in between anguish and anxiety. Our silence reveals to others the depth of our woundedness; they see us as the victim of circumstances. But in our hearts we know that we are being obstinate and deceptive. The rhythm of our life changes and becomes different. We develop a nervousness that we were once able to control.

The *third attitude* is welcoming. The welcoming of events supposes a control of our nerves and imagination. The objective of the absence of complaint is to help us welcome events be they happy or unhappy. In unhappy events, suffering remains just as acute but it is less devastating. By controlling our imagination and our nerves we can still ask questions: What is happening? What does God want to teach me by this event? What is he asking me to live? What is hidden in this event, in this unthinkable, unexpected situation? Suffering will help to sustain our faith and faith will establish itself in the midst of our confusion. We will feel less deprived. It takes time to find a solution to this enigma of suffering. At times the meaning of an event is clarified in a few days; at times only months or years later.

One Sunday, my brother and I went to the house of some friends to play. I was twelve years old and my brother was thirteen. Camille and Gerard could not come out; they were going out with their father. We went to visit some other friends; they were going fishing with their father. A third visit and we had the same results. Both of us were sad and we sat on the edge of the sidewalk our feet in the gutter, asking ourselves questions. We had lost our father nine years earlier. Why did God take our father? We too, on this lovely Sunday in spring, would have been with him and we would have been happy like our friends. At supper, alone with our mother and a younger sister, we asked the question: why did God come and take our father? He knew we needed him. My mother answered: My poor children, I suffer as much as you do from this separation. Often I too have asked myself the same question. Why? Why? But I have never found the answer. If one day God gives it to me I will pass it on to you.

Thirteen years after this conversation, I celebrated my first Mass before my family. I was happy to be a priest and all my family were thanking God with me. After thanksgiving my mother asked: "Do you remember the question that you asked me one day. If you are interested, I received the answer during Mass. If your father had lived, you would not have become a priest. Your father was a business-man, he was a success in all that he attempted. He was proud of his two sons. He would have drawn you into the whirlwind of his activities. He had little attraction for studies and you would have started work very young. If God chose you to be his priest, he had to open up the way for you and he did. To be a priest is a great gift, my son, but it's very costly. It was 22 years later that the meaning of this enigma was clarified for my mother.

It is here that the *absence of complaint* plays an important role. It disciplines the heart, fortifies our faith, gives us a certain self-control, help us to focus our sights on God who submitted his own Son to the caprices of events.

Every reasonable creature is conditioned by events. Jesus himself led an earthly life that was turned upside down by often unforeseeable events. Events caused him to be born in a cave in Bethlehem instead of in a cradle at Nazareth; they caused him to grow up in exile, to travel to Judea, Samaria and Galilee. His voyages, his teaching, his style, his manners were all conditioned by events. An event is a sealed envelope; it must be opened if we are to discover the will of God in it.

Those who endeavor to avoid complaint develop a great gentleness of heart. They benefit from a grace that we can call the *courtesy of the Holy Spirit* which infuses into the hearts of those who love a gentle way of thinking, acting and reacting.

Events play a considerable role in human life. In order not to be broken, we must learn to read the messages that they carry. Events condition everyone's existence: today we are in one place, tomorrow in another. Events move us and transport us from one part of the world to another. We must believe that the smallest event of the day as well as the most serious event of our lives speaks its own language which we can learn to understand.

The *absence of complaint* is the key to the enigma concealed in every event. All is providential. Jesus said, I wish no harm to anyone but I want all to be converted.

Everything should draw us closer to God, the active source of our being. He makes us flexible through the pressure of events. Place, time, temperature, climate, the occupation of others — everything affects and conditions us. We must admit it and accept a certain measure of dependency. Events speak and the absence of complaint disposes us to listen. It is not a matter of analyzing events to find their causes but rather to grasp the sense of the message that they bring. We must recall this proverb from Holy Scripture: "*The fear of the Lord is the beginning of knowledge; wisdom and instruction fools despise.*" (Prv 1:7)

Fear of the Lord is not a troubling fear, nor a fear that terrorizes. It is a sensitivity of heart in the presence of God seen as a Father full of goodness and tenderness, slow to anger, having unlimited mercy. This sensitivity is heightened when we avoid complaint and criticism. It becomes a principle of wisdom and even contributes to forming us in wisdom. (cf. Prv 9:10; 15:33) Protected by the absence of complaint, sensitivity calms us, creates a favorable climate for reflection and is truly a gentleness of heart, a tenderness expressed in peace.

If we are capable of thinking of God, of nourishing ourselves with his presence, of avoiding criticism and complaint, it is because we are filled with the Holy Spirit and have recognized that we are beings of service. Then we can say with Jesus: "*I did not come to be served but to serve...*" (Mt 20:28) The height of friendship is to give our lives for those we love: "*No one has greater love than this, to lay down one's life for one's friends. You are my friends if you do what I command you.*" (Jn 15:13-14)

Being of Service

If we truly want to encounter the Lord, it is not enough to place ourselves in his presence, we must also live as Jesus lived. On many occasions Jesus refers us to the will of his Father. At least fourteen times in the Gospel he tells us that he is attached above all to the will of He who sent him among us. Jesus clearly and precisely demonstrates that service and the choice of last place are the means of attracting his Spirit and of acquiring the Gospel way of living.

We will become persons of service when we recognize that the Holy Spirit is a living being who inhabits us; when, following the example of Jesus, we devote ourselves body and soul to the will of the Father. Then the Holy Spirit will create a new heart for us: a heart of flesh instead of a heart of stone which ignores all that belongs to true friendship.

To get a better grasp of the substantial difference that exists between the accomplishment of an occasional act of service and the service lived by those whose are endowed with faculties and mechanisms totally oriented toward service, it is good right from the beginning to give a descriptive definition of each individual term. Therefore, we will define a "*being*," a "*service*," and a "*being of service.*" As attempts that have been successful, we will use the example of two Secular Institutes approved and encouraged by the Church. Finally, we will conclude by contemplating Jesus who shows himself to us as a being of service and invites us to follow him.

1. Terminology

a) *Being*

A *being* is a living, active, intelligent, reasonable person, endowed with a free will, having an exceptional capacity to act, to love, to accept the love of others, to understand, to listen, to express his ideas and to respect others. Someone who is able to maturely assume serious responsibilities. This person, created in the image and likeness of God, is endowed with numerous positive qualities i.e.: natural gifts, talents, aptitudes, attractions, energies and dynamisms, as well as with a free will, that unique faculty which permits each of us to determine our choices.

Among all earthly creatures, we are the only ones who can say "yes" or "no" to whatever happens or to any person. Endowed with a conscience, which is like a videocassette, recording the moral value of memories, thoughts, desires and deliberate acts, we assume the burden for illogical, brutal or senseless responses. The conscience feels comfortable with what is good; it is tormented when involved in evil: when it cheats or when it deviates from good. The conscience is only free when it is in peace.

Claude Robert Eatherby, a young American pilot, was only 24 years old when they ordered him to drop the atomic bomb on the city of Hiroshima. He did not see the bomb explode on August 6, 1945 but in the days that followed, he saw the devastation caused by the bomb and his nerves broke. For 33 years — until his death in July of 1978 — he was never able to free himself from guilt and for 15 years he slept very little. The stress became so overpowering that he became mute in the last years of his life in Houston, Texas.

His brother James tells us that for years Claude Robert walked back and forth both day and night saying that his brain was on fire and that he could see the Japanese of Hiroshima dying in a furnace. (Houston, 7-7-78)

Conscience is often a mirror that reflects a brutal truth. If this truth is not assimilated, it destroys a human being by torturing him with remorse. Claude Robert acted in response to an order given him by his commanders. Still, the resulting brutality was so sudden and so horrible that his brain could not tolerate it.

Living beings that come forth from the hands of the Creator can become children of God through baptism. This sacrament enriches them with incomparable supernatural capacities and makes them powerful enough to reach the summit of perfection which will always remain an enigma for the majority of persons.

As living beings who play such a marvelous part in the divine plan we must, nevertheless, accept to be of service and to freely submit our will to God who, without using physical violence, gives us a precise commandment which allows for no ambiguity. *"You shall love the Lord your God with all your heart, with all your soul, with all your mind, and with all your strength.* (Mk 12:30-31)

In order to be reasonable, we must recognize that all our qualities, faculties and powers, all the mechanisms within us that make us unique beings are free gifts from God; they are special charisms that must be used as instruments of service.

As reasonable beings we must naturally be on the side of God, especially if we are baptized and consecrated, privileged children of God. Built to be dependent, we will gradually discover our full potential by becoming aware of our positive possibilities and the mechanisms of power within ourselves, and by being in communion with God who has made us administrators (not proprietors) of so many gifts, talents, tendencies and goods freely given to us.

A reasonable person is a work of art, an authentic representation of God. In his divine plan, God created us for service. He gave us a remarkable intelligence, will, sensibility and depth, and even a marvelous physical body. We can aim at the heights of perfection insofar as we accept our mission of service.

b) *Service*

The word *"serve"* is taken from a Latin word meaning: to be a slave, to be submissive or devoted. This word frightens us when it relates to a relationship of inferiority with masters inclined to abuse their powers or when it indicates certain persons in authority who do not have enough discernment to recognize that they must command not in their own name but in the name of God who has given them a mandate.

Often, we seem to accept this authority, but we are high strung, our nerves are on edge and we grumble, not because of what we are asked to do but because of the way in which a command or an order is given. Our defense mechanisms are delicate, subtle and reveal our limitations of impatience, egoism and self-love.

The word *"serve"* — that we accept at least in theory — also has other meanings, but none of them free us from those who have authority over us. Each meaning describes the necessity of submitting, of taking the last place, of deferring to others and of serving.

The dictionaries Robert and Larousse affirm that *to serve* is to sustain someone we want to help. It is to carry out certain obligations towards those whom we must obey; it is to aid someone by supporting their credibility, favoring them, being available and useful to them; it is being open to the needs of others. It is also to place ourselves at the disposition of others: to give, offer, present. It means to willingly and freely be instruments in the hands of others.

c) *Beings of Service*

To become *beings of service,* we must recognize our strengths and be sensitive to the example that Jesus brings us regarding his Father. We must pray much and labor to study the behavior and conduct of Jesus, who in the eyes of his Father, succeeded in living his life as Messiah better than any union leader struggling for the demands of others whether they are just or not. The more Jesus is experientially accepted, the more that service in his name will appear possible, logical and satisfying.

A being of service is an intelligent being who willingly and freely stands on the side of God, who strives to be a docile instrument of his will, as soon as this will is known.

When Joshua grew old, he gathered together at Shechem all the elders, leaders, judges and scribes of the tribes of Israel. As he addressed them, he tried, first of all, to help them become aware of the Lord's goodness to them; then he strictly warned them against tepidity and weakness. Finally, he tried to convince them of the necessity of serving God above all. Joshua — burning with fervor, overflowing with eloquence — calls upon all the Israelites to bind themselves to God alone:

> If it does not please you to serve the Lord, choose today whom you wish to serve, the gods that your ancestors served beyond the River or the gods of

the Amorites in whose country you are now dwelling. As for me and my household, we will serve the Lord." (Jos 24:15)

Won over by the word and example of Joshua, the people solemnly swore to serve only the Lord, and to unconditionally put aside their idols. On that day, the people of Israel recognized once more that in the thought of God they are a *people of service* who prefigure all the believers in the world. To believe in God is to dispose ourselves to follow the commandments, to put them into practice each day of our lives, and to imitate the example of Jesus.

Jesus is the most perfect model of *a being of service.* He encourages us to follow him by asking us to aim for perfection because his heavenly Father is perfect. Walking in the footsteps of Jesus, we rediscover Mary — his mother and ours — the apostles, and the successive generations of committed Christians from all parts of the world. The Church is *a being of service*; communities, societies, institutes, families, and individuals are all *beings of service* in the plan of God. Each group, as well as each individual, must try to define and insert themselves into their special place in the Church.

Jesus, a living person, attaches himself to each of us. He makes himself the marvelous link that binds us to one another in the same love and the same sense of service. He moves us to generously seize the thoughts, desires and will of his Father, so that we may truly become the *beings of service* that the Church expects us to be.

2. We Must Define Ourselves as Beings of Service

Here I would like to give you the example of two Secular Institutes; their manner of expression will surely help each group or each individual to think of themselves and to describe themselves as beings of service.

a) *The Voluntas Dei Institute*

This institute is well-defined by its name: *Voluntas Dei*, two Latin words that mean "the Will of God." The founding of this Institute was suggested to me at the end of February 1958 by Father Leo Deschatelets, then superior general of the Oblates of Mary Immaculate, at the Oblate Mission House in Montreal. To my way of thinking, this foundation was the will of God expressed through legitimate authority. As the result of a series of providential events, I asked myself why each member of this Institute could not be a concrete sign of the will of God, a being of service.

A member of this Institute is, above all else, one consecrated to seeking, adhering to and carrying out God's will. The five attitudes, used to encounter Jesus and to assimilate his life, rapidly created in the Institute's young founders a mentality of suppleness, simplicity, mutual aid and fraternity.

In their Constitutions they describe themselves as *persons of service*: "...accepting all acts of devotedness asked for by legitimate authority; being faithful to their responsibilities, and always being of service by training themselves to respond to every request." This simple article reveals the distinctive quality that characterizes the members of the Institute as people who have attained a certain maturity, who have a sense of responsibility, the desire to seek the will of God and the assurance that, as servants of the Church and respectful collaborators of legitimate ecclesiastical and civil authority, they stand with God.

Thanks to this spirit which characterizes the person of service, members of the Institute become adults faithful to their commitments and profoundly attached to the Church and to the authority that governs them, even on the level of the Institute. The members of the Institute Voluntas Dei develop their adhesion to the will of God especially by cultivating a spirit of recollection, humility and fraternal charity.

In 1958, the year the Institute was founded, I had deliberately chosen the term "will of God" to indicate each individual member of the Institute. I rejoiced to see the young men giving themselves with such ardor and generosity and I said to myself as I looked at each one: he is truly a "*Voluntas Dei*," i.e., a concrete, visible manifestation of the will of God. With enthusiasm I watched the growth of these young men who came from all the corners of the earth: Canada, United States, Sri Lanka, Haiti, France, India, Laos... for me each one was a living, active, loving, and present "will of God." This appellation responded to the needs of my faith; I found it suggestive, fulfilling, and inspiring.

The Church asked us to call the group of young men "*The Voluntas Dei Institute*" instead of simply "*Voluntas Dei.*" We accepted the desire of the Church as a will of God.

Nevertheless, we can say that each member, in the depths of his heart, strives to merit the title "Voluntas Dei" because the Church has chosen us to be persons of service.

b) *The O.M.M.I.'s and the Volunteers of God*

The Oblate Missionaries of Mary Immaculate also strongly express their belonging to Jesus through the quality of their being of service. The word "Oblate" means offering. The Oblate is an offering that Mary Immaculate constantly presents to Jesus. She is an commissioned offering to which a specific mission has been assigned.

To give more emphasis to the quality of their attachment to God, the first 500 Oblates each chose an attribute of the Virgin Mary which they inserted into the motto of the Institute: the Charity of Christ through Mary Immaculate. For example, one lived the charity of Christ through Mary of Peace, another through Mary Mediatrix, another through Mary of the Sacred Heart, etc... It seems that linked to Mary their model, their alliance with Christ as *a being of service* was more thoughtful, more conscientious, more practical and more attached to the present moment.

The Oblate must serve wherever Christ has his rights. We can find her in all types of milieu, in all trades, in all climates, wherever the Church needs witnesses of love, beings of service. We must not be surprised therefore if she is in 25 countries: in Asia, in South America, in Africa, in Europe and in North America. They are also in communist countries; nothing stops their zeal. They are efficacious insofar as they remain in the spirit of their five attitudes which they call their five points: the distinguishing characteristic of their fervor and their dynamism.

The Oblate is Mary's offering to the heart of Jesus; she is a gift prepared by the Holy Spirit, to bring about in the Church a special way of serving the world, of living in the midst of the world like a leaven of generosity, simplicity and spontaneity.

In a spirit of faith, the Oblate cooperates in the plan of salvation by accepting — according to her strength and possibilities — the acts of devotedness requested by legitimate authority. She works with the Lord and with her brothers and sisters in the construction of a new world by accomplishing her temporal tasks in a spirit of constant availability so as to manifest in peace and joy the love by which God loves the world. This availability which commits her whole life to the service of others, identifies her with Christ who perfectly followed the will of his Father.

The Oblate, *a being of service,* identifies herself with Jesus, endeavoring to imitate his conduct towards the Father, accepting to collaborate with suppleness and submission in the work of Redemption and the plan of salvation. She puts her entire availability, with her strengths and her potentialities, into accepting and carrying out all acts of devoted-ness indicated to her by legitimate authority.

Endowed with a sense of responsibility, the Oblate accomplishes her personal tasks, lives in a state of constant availability and manifests, by living as a being of service, that peace and joy which are the fruits of the Holy Spirit and the evident signs of the Father's love for each of us. Moreover, the Oblate never seeks to be isolated or to work alone. Rather, inspired by the thought and example of Jesus, she remains united to her sisters and to all others concerned with building a new world.

In the countries where they work, the Oblates have drawn together a considerable number of laity of all ages, forming them into groups of committed Christians called the *Volunteers of God.* Each day these people live the experience of the five atti-tudes, or the five points. These laypeople, spread throughout many countries, make a formal prom-ise each year to consciously, willingly and freely live the five attitudes in order to be sowers of peace, harmonious and pacific elements in the world and builders of serenity.

3. The Thought and Example of Jesus: a Being of Service

Jesus abandoned himself to the service of his Father with complete confidence; he gave himself unconditionally. He was attached to the Father like a stream is attached to its source, like rays draw their brilliance from the sun. He admitted that his vocation of God-Man came from his Father; that his thoughts, desires and actions were under the inspiration of the Father. He affirmed that his submission was to be taken seriously. It was not limited only to the spirit but it engaged all his activity, directed his whole life, presided over his death, and continued in the resurrection and in the sending of the Spirit who completes his gift.

Let's take time to meditate the words of Jesus who reveals the depths of his heart to us and demonstrates the absolute dependency of his being, fully disposed to carry out his Father's least desire. Among the apostles, it is John — so close to Jesus for a number of years — who points out the reflexes of his Master whom he presents to the world as *a being of service.*

"My food is to do the will of the One who sent me and to finish his work." (Jn 4:34)

"I cannot do anything on my own; I judge as I hear, and my judgement is just, because I do not seek my own will but the will of the One who sent me." (Jn 5:30)

"...because I came down from heaven not to do my own will but the will of the One who sent me." (Jn 6:38)

"When you lift up the Son of Man, then you will realize that I AM, and that I do nothing on my own, but I say only what the Father taught me. The One who sent me is with me. He has not left me alone, because I always do what is pleasing to him." (Jn 8:28-29)

"...the ruler of the world is coming. He has no power over me but the world must know that I love the Father and that I do just as the Father has commanded me." (Jn 14:30-31)

"As the Father loves me, so I also love you. Remain in my love. If you keep my commandments, you will remain in my love, just as I have kept my Father's commandments and remain in his love. I have told you this so that my joy might be in you and your joy might be complete." (Jn 15:9-11)

If we take time to reflect on Jesus and his way of recognizing his dependence on the Father, we will be profoundly touched by his attitudes and perhaps we would become more deeply conscious of this truth: we must behave towards Jesus as he behaved towards the Father. If he claims to have received all freely from the Father, what are we to conclude? *"What do you possess that you have not received? But if you have received it, why are you boasting as if you did not receive it?"* (1 Cor 4:7)

Therefore, we must admit candidly that God created human beings to become *beings of service.* We must practice a certain humility accepting God as the Principle of our being, the sustenance of our existence, the Pinnacle from which we take flight and rediscover our rhythm as children of God.

When we pray to the Lord in the secret of our room we are not tempted to lie; the truth flows forth from our hearts with humility and spontaneity. Jesus often prayed to the Father in secret. For thirty years he lived at home with Mary and Joseph in obscure villages of Egypt or in Nazareth. We would think that at certain moments he must have suffered from being confined within such narrow boundaries. We have difficulty seeing ourselves attached to our home for thirty years, practicing a seemingly monotonous trade. We could say that at the beginning of his public life he felt the need to know that his Father was thinking about him. The heavens open twice to publicly allow the word of the Father to come through. When he is baptized by John the Baptist, witnesses hear a voice say: "*You are my beloved Son; with you I am well pleased.*" (Lk 3:22) And one day when Jesus is transfigured before three of his apostles, this same voice repeats the same terms, adding: "*...listen to him.*"

To pray in a natural, relaxed manner, there is nothing better than solitude; Jesus often goes aside to pray. (cf. Mk 6:46) One day Simon Peter sets off to find Jesus; in the early hours of the morning he discovers him in a deserted place in prayer. (cf. Mk 1:35) Before choosing from among his disciples the twelve who would become the pillars of his Church, Jesus goes alone to the mountain to spend the night in prayer to his Father. (cf. Lk 6:12) One day, Jesus is in prayer surrounded by his disciples; he asks them: "*Who do people say I am?*" Peter, in this atmosphere of prayer, lets the Holy Spirit speak through him. (cf. Lk 9:18-20)

Jesus teaches his disciples to pray, so that their faith will not fail, so that they will have the power to drive out a special kind of demons, so that they learn to be submissive; submission is the backbone of service. (cf. Mt 6:6ff.)

Jesus envelops us in the force and charm of his personality. Even though his prayers are frequently addressed to the Father to whom he is totally abandoned, he does not forget us and he wants each of us to participate in his same glory.

In chapter 17 of John's Gospel, we find Jesus placing himself between the Father and us, to bind us together and to make us all one:

> "I glorified you on earth, by accomplishing the work that you gave me to do... I revealed your name to those whom you gave me out of the world. They belonged to you, and you gave them to me, and they have kept your word. ...the words you gave to me I have given to them, and they accepted them and truly understood that I came from you, and they have believed that you sent me. I pray for...the ones you have given me, because they are yours, and everything of mine is yours and everything of yours is mine and I have been glorified in them. Holy Father, keep those that you have given me in your name, so that they may be one just as we are one." (Jn 17:4-11)

To Jesus' way of thinking we must be prayerful, submissive people, servants, beings of service. These are the conditions necessary if he is to absorb us into an intense union with himself and bind us to the Father. Jesus is a being of service. He states in all simplicity that he is but a docile instrument of the Father, that he has received everything from him, that all he is and has, all he thinks and does, all that he teaches comes from the Father. This is his strength, the extraordinary dimension of his personality in regard to service. We must pass through him to reach the Father; we must acquire his mentality of being submissive, of being servant which He sums up thusly:

> "Just so, the Son of Man did not come to be served but to serve and to give his life as ransom for many." (Mt 20:28)

> "I am among you as the one who serves." (Lk 22:27)

> "The Father will honor whoever serves me." (Jn 12:26)

> "If I, therefore, the master and teacher, have washed your feet, you ought to wash one another's feet. (Jn 13:14)

Even though he is dependent on the Father, Jesus is relaxed and serene, full of life and vigor in serving others. He promises this same liberation to all those who model themselves on his example. *"I live and you will live."* (Jn 14:19) *"The words I have spoken to you are spirit and life."* (Jn 6:63) *"Whoever keeps my word will never see death."* (Jn 8:51) *"I came so they might have life..."* (Jn 10:10)

It is in following the example of Jesus that we will accomplish what the Lord asks of each of us.

Therefore, we must hate our own life, i.e., sacrifice our own way of thinking which is not always in conformity with the plan of God. (cf. Lk 14:26) To lose our life is to offer it with love to the Lord. (cf. Jn 12:27) It is to sacrifice it totally in the service of those we love. (cf. Jn 15:13)

4. We Are Invited to Model Our Lives on Jesus

"Master, to whom shall we go? You have the words of eternal life." (Jn 6:68) He will not let us fall, we will have our quota of happiness and he will give us the necessary energy and dynamism. Let us set to work then and strive to live intensely the present moment. Thus we will eventually familiarize ourselves with the mentality of Jesus. We will explore his way of thinking, grasp his motivations, comprehend the sense of his luminous words and walk with him in intimacy.

To accelerate our rhythm, we will be assiduous in carrying out our exercises of piety each day in order to keep the sacred fire of fervor burning. We will never become professionals in serving until we have had a lived experience of Jesus, until we feel his living, active, moving presence within us, until we look upon him as our best friend — he to whom we can tell all and who has the liberty of determining and influencing our choices. We will be amateurs who work sporadically, and when our motivation cools down, we will end up by giving shoddy, indifferent, apathetic service.

Rivers are imposing and majestic as long as their flow is abundant and generous. It is the same for beings of service. They are true and efficacious as long as they are nourished by the presence of God, the spirit of prayer and regularity in carrying out certain exercises of piety. As long as they frequent the sacraments and dip into the other sources that the Church puts at the disposition of her children.

Not only should we dwell upon the life of Christ, scrutinizing it carefully, we must also endeavor to discover this life in others. It is impossible to be a being of service if we ignore others. We must first of all be attentive to those who are invested with the power of authority; we must be respectful and attentive. These people are channels by which God sends us his grace. Therefore, we cannot organize our lives alone, go promenading throughout the world letting ourselves be guided uniquely by our creativity and imagination. We must stop, take time to discover the obligations of our chosen state and accept them freely.

As *beings of service,* we must realize that the vocation of a Christian is exigent, that it implies discipline and a serious formation.

Each time we render a service to another, it is God who is served. (cf. Mt 25:35ff) Each time we give ourselves to others we resemble the Author of all good. To render a service and to accept all acts of devotedness is a way of giving our lives to the service of members of the great human family. It is a mark of friendship that causes the heart to celebrate.

Christians, conscious of the role they have to play in the plan of God, seek to become more perfect and to discover new talents, new aptitudes and powerful energies within themselves. They seriously analyze their dynamism to reactivate their optimism and enthusiasm. Inactivity, a lack of responsibility, frequent unemployment and laziness destroy more human beings than deadly wars. Beings of service are never inert, never on strike. They feel responsible, alive and endowed with abilities that enable them to help others.

To serve is good for the normal evolution of our personality, our character and our whole being. To accept to serve, to officially recognize ourselves as beings of service is an indication of psychological, moral and spiritual health. If we cease recognizing our possibilities to serve, we become sleepers, dreamers. The world comes to us insofar as it discovers us to be supple, simple and fraternal; thus we can create durable friendships.

In addition to what the Church gives us through the liturgy and the sacraments, we must dedicate time to meditating, praying, reading the Bible and participating in communitarian, family or team meetings. Thus we will become more accessible to others and much more open and welcoming.

Taking the example of Jesus, we will go to others without letting ourselves be blocked by the grimness of their character or by the mystery of their spiritual journey. Jesus, prototype of the *being of service*, invites us to imitate his technique for making contacts. He frequented intellectuals: Nicodemus, Simon the Leper, Joseph of Arimathea; and he frequented people whose reputations left something to be desired, but who wanted to change: Mary Magdalene, the Samaritan woman, the woman caught in adultery, one of the two thieves on the cross. He accepts to visit them and to allow them to join the group of people who love him enough to form bonds of friendship with him: Lazarus, Zaccheus, Jairus, the widow of Naim, the centurion, etc... He manages to live and create unity among the apostles, all unique individuals: Peter, at times exalted and disconcerting; Judas, secretive and dishonest; Thomas, over-sensitive and argumentative, James, violent and drastic, whom Jesus calls a son of thunder.

If we keep our eyes open, we will not lack occasions to serve. To serve is to live as Jesus did:

"For the kingdom of God is not a matter of food and drink, but of righteousness, peace and joy in the Holy Spirit. Whoever serves Christ in this way is pleasing to God and approved by others. Let us then pursue what leads to peace and to building up one another." (Rom 14:17-19)

"... learn from me for I am meek and humble of heart." (Mt 11:29)

Sower of Peace

The Christian must endeavor to become a *sower of peace*. Peace must be one of the things we seek most assiduously. Conscious of thinking, speaking and acting under the guidance of the Holy Spirit, the person of service moves towards a peace that is durable, because it is authenticated each day.

Peace is a gift of God, a mature fruit produced by love. The evangelist Matthew places peace at the summit of the Beatitudes: *"Blessed are the peacemakers for they will be called children of God."* (Mt 5:9) By nature and through grace, Christians are children of God, but as we build peace we become more aware of our belonging to God, of our depending on him as our Father, as well as on his ability to transform each of us. The sower of peace realizes that he is in a state of evolution and transformation. Peace is truly the summit of the spiritual journey; it is the pinnacle of a pyramid whose foundation is the presence of God.

Sowers of peace lean on the rock of their being which God has chosen as a temple of his Spirit. Peace is the life of God flowing into us which is experienced as a benediction; this benediction engenders in us the faculty of being aware of God in all circumstances, and in the presence of any person or event. It is the quality of the presence of God and of an extant peace which gives a being of service the consciousness of a daily mission to be carried out. Peace is the most tangible manifestation of the active presence of God, of submission to a Supreme Being, of the heart's being possessed by the One whom we consider a marvelous, attentive and gracious Father.

In order to better understand this fifth attitude — *sower of peace* — which should give others the deepest quality of Christian witness, I will explain the term, *sower of peace.* I will give different definitions of peace, what it requires, and what it expects of us.

1. Terminology

A *sower of peace* is someone who puts all their energies and ardor into avoiding useless emotional and sentimental problems and avoiding the idle confidences which ordinarily turn into criticisms and complaints, sowing uneasiness and remorse.

Sowers of peace concentrate above all on the positive aspects of others, seeking patiently to detect their qualities, gifts, talents, aptitudes, attractions and energies. Their hearts radiate enough tenderness to love others, to excuse them, to pardon them when necessary and to serve them with simplicity and humility.

Following the Lord's bidding, *sowers of peace* are more concerned with making changes in themselves by renouncing certain ideas or by accepting the disturbances caused by others, than with controlling and alienating others and forcing them to live according to their own customs and habits.

Sowers of peace keep watch over the value of their motivations, seeking to imitate Jesus in his way of dealing with his contemporaries. They tend to avoid evil, to do good, to control their tongue, to keep guard over their lips, to construct and spread peace, to sow it in their milieu and in the hearts of others.

As good Pope Jean XXIII tells us, the *sower of peace* has a talent for not complicating simple things, and for simplifying complicated things. They manage to reduce the mountains, built by our deformed imaginations, into the molehills that they are.

St. Paul describes the sower of peace in his letter to the Corinthians. (cf. 1 Cor 13) Love is a generator of peace. If love fails, peace disappears. As love grows stronger, peace becomes more resistant, visible and active. Even if we possess all human power and have every talent which characterizes the geniuses of every discipline and even if we were gratified by having the preternatural gifts which adorned our first parents before their fall, if we have no love we would be nothing before God. Why not meditate slowly St. Paul's text explaining charity. Substitute your name for that of love. Instead of saying: love is patient, love serves, love is not jealous, love is never boastful or conceited, simply say: I, such and such a person, am patient, serve, etc. I will conclude that if I, a sower of peace, have not love, I am but a clashing cymbal.

If you carry this reflection to its logical conclusion, you will conclude, as I did, that it is necessary to live as fully as possible our capacities to love God and our neighbor. Our hearts must be filled with love; we must be enveloped in love, robed in peace since in God's plan we are destined to spread peace, to give witness to it. This is the road on which Jesus leads those who love him and who believe in him.

Even if we do our best, there will always be those who judge us unfavorably as they did Jesus. Some will understand us; others will pass alongside us and ignore us. Still others will fight us because they consider our ideas strange. The Pharisees, the Scribes, the Sadducees not only shut their eyes in order not to discover the fundamental qualities of Jesus but by well-orchestrated propaganda, they blocked the way for multitudes in the Old Testament, closing off all access to the New Testament which told about the life of Jesus, his doctrine of goodness, his hope. In their collective blindness, they saw Jesus as a simple prophet who merited the sort of his forerunners, an atrocious, inconceivable death without a just trial. The Pharisees were only a handful of people, but they succeeded in placing obstacles in the path of the people who would have given themselves to Jesus: God, Redeemer, Savior, Prince of Peace, as Isaiah called him centuries before his arrival on earth.

Sowers of peace do not allow themselves to be troubled; neither illness, infirmities, nor exterior humiliations, neither riches, aridities, distractions, temptations, nor novelties can draw them away

116

from the style of life that Jesus extolled in the Gospel. They do not ask themselves troubling questions; they live by faith; they abandon themselves to God and they become aware of him each day. Thus the present moment becomes a place of friendly encounters.

Sowers of peace put their energy into sowing calm, tranquility, and order. Nothing troubles them neither interiorly nor exteriorly. They have confidence in others and are ready to form alliances that bring about durable friendships. (cf. Nm 25:12) They are heralds of harmony and union; by their whole being they favor team, family or fraternal life.

The *sower of peace* is endowed with two fundamental faculties. The *first faculty* is static, it is an unshakable rock: indestructible, durable, solid: *Jesus himself is the source of that peace.* He instills the Holy Spirit in the heart of each Christian to remain as the eternally living One. Thus the Holy Spirit abides in us by his life, his thought, his creativity, his efficacy and his love. We know that the Holy Spirit is in the heart of each Christian, but it is necessary to think of him often. That is why Jesus himself asks us to pray without ceasing.

The *second faculty* is dynamic. Love produces an important fruit called peace. When we say that someone is an element of peace, we are simply affirming that we have discovered the solidity of this person, the quality of God that can be perceived in him and the delicacy of his witness. Also, when we say that someone is a builder of peace, we avow that we have discovered the quality of dynamism in this person, a way of creating, edifying and

117

propagating peace in order to give others the security of a true, solid and quiet joy. When we refer to someone as a sower of peace, we are saying that this person is filled with peace — here is the static aspect — and that he infuses others with the desire for peace — here is the dynamic aspect.

2. Definition of Peace

The word "*peace*" is as ambiguous as the word "*love*" which we use to describe all kinds of situations; we give it a wide range of meanings. I will begin first of all by giving the thought of Vatican II on peace. Then we will reflect together, seeking definitions that describe what we have lived in our experiences with the Lord. With the Second Vatican Council we will speak of what it is not and then we will insist on what it is.

a) *What Peace Is Not*

"*Peace is not merely the absence of war. Nor can it be reduced solely to the maintenance of a balance of power between enemies. Nor is it brought about by dictatorship.*" (Gaudium et Spes, no. 78)

Peace is not an arms race; it is not a cold war where each side remains rooted in their own position; nor is it an accumulation of atomic weapons which inspire fear, respect and even terror.

For individuals, peace must not be equated with indifference, coldness or keeping our distance from people that we cannot ignore, even if we do not feel the least attraction, sympathy or friendship for them.

Have you ever leafed through a family album? You surely stopped to examine people you knew. Have you noticed that each face provokes different feelings in you? Some are agreeable to look at; they awaken happy memories and warm sentiments. We suddenly become effusive, gesticulating to manifest the true joy that these memories evoke. We realize that these people still remain in our hearts, that we remember them with pleasure, that their memory stirs up emotions in us.

When we look at other faces we turn the pages more quickly. We only have vague remembrances of them which are neither disagreeable nor agreeable. We never took the time to detect their qualities.

Finally we get to photos of other people that provoke discomfort or even repulsion; unconsciously we reject them. We refuse to accept them unconditionally; their faces disturb us and upset our emotions. We feel aggressive, harsh words rise up in us, our faces tighten: all this happens almost unconsciously. We relive past problems; we find within ourselves an animosity that we thought we had left behind.

Each time we see the same photos we have the same emotional reactions; the years keep passing, but the sentiments of hurt remain just as violent. We should not allow all these toxins of suffering and these negative remembrances to remain within us. We demolish ourselves each time we are agitated by them; then we are no longer sowers of peace.

We will never attain peace by sending others to the devil, or by pretending to ignore them. It is not by saying "Leave me in peace" that I obtain peace nor by saying "Go away, I no longer want to see you." that I will feel free. Moreover, if we really want to merit the title "sower of peace," we must go beyond the simple purification of our memories. We must become capable one day of leafing through our family album and stopping to look with interest at each face, feeling relaxed and sympathetic, without any danger of disturbing our self-control.

Peace must be more than a sentiment of good humor. It must be an awareness that a superior presence abides in us, that the Holy Spirit has complete liberty in sensitizing us to his gifts, charisms, and fruits. That under his inspiration, we are able to develop an empathy with others and to accumulate within ourselves images that will create wondrous presences which will populate our memories with positive, relaxing remembrances. Then we will discover that our hearts are capable of affection, tenderness, goodness, amiability, and indulgence.

b) *What Peace Is*

Peace is a fruit of justice, love and fraternity. Its source is Christ himself. From the moment of his birth in Bethlehem, heaven became the scene of harmonious song helping us to discover the Great Sower of peace, the Gatherer of all those who are avid for peace; "*Glory to God in the highest and on earth peace to those on whom his favor rests.*" (Lk 2:14)

Jesus recruited his *sowers of peace* from all classes of society. He imposed on them an energetic discipline so that they could journey towards the conquest of peace without tiring. Peace, like fire, remains effective insofar as we take care of it. Those "on whom his favor rests" are the Apostles, the disciples whom Jesus liked to call his sheep. Those "on whom his favor rests" are all those who call on his wisdom, his power, his goodness, his mercy. They are the poor, the handicapped, the ill, the deprived who listen to him and follow him.

In the thought of Jesus, all disciples are a presence of peace, if they consent to abandon all to follow him (cf. Mt 8:19-22), if they accept to carry his cross (cf. Mt 10:38), if they strive to know the truth that will make them free (cf. Jn 8:31), if they endeavor to serve their brothers and sisters, their neighbors (cf. Mt 20:28), if they trust themselves wholeheartedly to Providence (cf. Mt 6:25), if they do not demand special treatment, if they accept not to be treated better than the master (cf. Mt 10:24), Jesus promises the sower of peace an eternal reward. (cf. Mt 19:29)

We will never arrive at the dimensions of true peace unless we are grafted onto Jesus. Never forget that he is the vine and we are the branches; we cannot live without his sap without the risk of drying up. The branch attached to a vine is healthy, insofar as the graft is solid and allows the sap which gives it life and dynamism to flow through it. United to Jesus, we can support many trials, we can take many risks, and we have the assurance that peace will not leave our hearts.

The peace that Jesus transmits to each of us cost him his incarnation, his life, his death, his resurrection, the redemption. As *sowers of peace*, we can thus recognize his works, because the goodness of the grape depends on the health of the vine and on the submissiveness of the branches.

Jesus, magnanimous and powerful source of peace, was sent into the midst of the world by his Father to recruit for heaven. He is the one who prepares a marvelous home for each of us. There we shall be proprietors, while still remaining submissive to he who gratifies us by his generosity.

By vocation we are *sowers* and *distributors of peace*. God truly placed in each of us a river of peace whose source is Jesus. It is up to us to manifest it, and to witness to this peace by developing our capacity to love, to be attentive, to show our magnanimity, and to have confidence in others. If we recognize our potential for peace, self-love will no longer have the power to upset our human relationships.

c) *Peace, a Fruit of Justice*

"Peace results from that harmony built into human society by its Divine Founder and actualized by men as they thirst after ever greater justice." (Gaudium et Spes, no. 78) The Council is speaking to every Christian in the world as well as to the heads of nations who have a mission to carry out. It addresses itself to all persons of good will, avid for good, and ready to better the world by leveling out the classes of society so that there will be less rich egoists on earth as well as fewer frustrated, bitter and discontented poor.

Each of us must seek to do something for the establishment of justice, first of all in ourselves and then in others. If we ourselves do not develop an acute sense of justice, we will never feel that we have a rigorous duty towards the underprivileged, the defenseless and the poor who may be living in misery. As *sowers of peace,* we must put aside that mentality of feeling comfortable in the midst of those who suffer. We must go a lot further than simply examining ourselves and asking ourselves questions.

In order for a fire to give light and heat, it must be constantly nourished, otherwise the darkness and cold will make it disappear. Peace follows the same law. It wastes away, it dwindles and disappears, if we do not kindle it daily. It is within us; we must not allow it to be put out; we must stand guard over its flame and begin again each time we are in the presence of the poor, the deprived, and the unloved.

Peace must be reconstructed every 24 hours; it is like a face that needs tireless and frequent care in order to preserve its youthfulness. Society, people, and events put our peace to the test at every moment; therefore, we must be vigilant, pray and act.

In chapter 32 verse 17, the prophet Isaiah affirms: "*Justice will bring about peace, right will produce calm and security.*" St. Augustine tells us that peace is tranquillity in order; it is both union and harmony; it is the repose that relaxes, the security that keeps away the terrors of a chaotic future caused by a disturbed society. Peace comes forth from a heart united to Jesus.

It is the presence of God and of peace that gives beings of service a consciousness of the mission that they must carry out here below. Peace is the most tangible manifestation of the active presence of God, and of the inspiration of the Holy Spirit.

d) *Peace, a Fruit of Love*

"*This peace cannot be obtained on earth unless we safeguard the well-being of others and, freely and trustingly share with one another the riches of our spirit and our talents... Hence, peace is likewise the fruit of love which goes beyond what simple justice can provide. That earthly peace which arises from love of our neighbor is both the symbol and the effect of the peace of Christ who comes forth from God the Father.*" (Gaudium et Spes, no. 78)

It is love which gives a true dimension to our relationships with God and others. It is love which stimulates us to respect the rights of others: the right to life, to subsistence, to a certain quota of material goods, to love and understanding, to a certain liberty, and to the confidence of others. Peace is the fruit of love. To love others is to look at them, to admire and respect them, to listen to them, to excuse and forgive them.

In July 1978 at Wimbleton, England, following a tennis tournament where the champions of the world had played against one another, a journalist, enthusiastic about the temperament of a young 22-year old man, Bjorn Borg, said: "Today the world of professional tennis is divided in two. On the one hand there is Bjorn Borg, a young Swede, world champion at Wimbleton for three successive years, and on the other hand, two or three hundred other players who work the international circuits. After his third successive victory, this young man is so far ahead that we need binoculars to see those who are following him: the Jimmy Connors, Guillermo Villas, the Ilie Nastase, the Vitas Gerulaitis." Why such a eulogy? Is this young man so phenomenal? Is he perhaps a superman? This enthusiasm was brought about partly by the superb quality of his game but even more by his force of concentration and above all by the richness of a personality that seeks to sow peace everywhere.

The same journalist describes Borg as a sower of peace; this is proven by his concentration and his respect for others. An English journalist made an amusing play on words with his name: Bjorn Borg

— an "ice-borg" so well was he able to concentrate on his game. He seemed to have no emotions, he plays a match as if it were a business deal. When he finishes a game he seems to come back down to earth. During a tournament we do not see his limits, he is absorbed by his game, he possesses all he needs: he is in good physical condition, he has great suppleness and rapidity, lightening reflexes and perfect control of his nerves. He never contests a shot nor a decision. He does not seek to irritate his adversary in order to make him lose his concentration. He respects everyone and never permits himself to insult them or even to say an unkind word to the crowds who at times harass him.

After a match, Borg seems to pull himself together in order to come back to reality and he willingly yields to the crowds of admirers and the numerous sports writers, welcoming them in spite of the repetitious and trite questions. (*Le Nouvelliste,* 12-7-78)

If this champion is so popular, if he has won the friendship of so many people, it is because he shows love for his neighbor by his delicate and attentive fashion of approaching people. The being of peace is vowed to respect, admire and pay attention to others.

In order to become champions in our profession of being a Christian, we too must pay attention to our concentration, that is, become aware that God is in us with his power, his riches, his gifts, his energies and that he uses us like polished instruments to live and distribute true peace each in our own milieu. We become sowers of peace insofar as we realize that God is the author of love and love is the generator of peace.

A *sower of peace* is someone who is conscious of being in love with God and neighbor, someone who builds and assembles, who is a worker, an artist, a practical person who knows his trade well. One who recognizes that God has chosen the Christian to be a temple of his Holy Spirit, and that he gives all that is needed: faculties, qualities, gifts, talents, aptitudes and charisms to establish, develop, propagate and distribute true peace to all.

Therefore, having so many riches, Christians are capable of creating amiable communications with others. This awareness that we are instruments helps us to place ourselves at the service of others: intelligence, heart, energy, dynamism, initiative and creativity. If Christians are not aware of their mission as builders of peace they will understand nothing of their supernatural vocation. If peace is the fruit of love, it becomes an incredible thread for binding ourselves to God for better or for worse. It frees us from all suspicion, from all rash judgement, from all wounded susceptibility, from all animosity, coldness or contestation in regard to our neighbor.

In each human being we can detect two very different sources of activity; the first source is God who brings forth true peace; the second source is self-love which brings forth conflict.

St. John Climacus, born around the year 525, learned to serve God at a very young age. At 16, inspired by the Holy Spirit, he retired alone into the desert to live a life of penance, prayer and solitude. The presence of God sustained him for the 40 years he lived at the foot of Mount Sinai. When he was 75 the hermits of the desert called him to become director general of all the monks. A man of prayer desirous of safeguarding peace in the hearts of all, he promised God to be a *sower of peace* and he encouraged his companions to do the same: by never beginning a discussion, by never contradicting anyone, by never arguing, by cultivating a spirit of recollection, by always looking at others with a spirit of friendship. John Climacus so impressed others by his wisdom that they were all more willing to listen to him than to launch out into the prattle of useless conversations. (*Vie des Saints,* Hugo Hoever)

3. Requirements for Peace

Peace requires all Christians to "*join with all true peacemakers in pleading for peace and bringing it about.*" (Gaudium et Spes, no. 78) The peace of a nation must begin in the heart of each individual. Peace is impossible if we do not feel the life of God in the center of our being. Peace will have the universal dimensions of charity when we feel the presence of God within ourselves, but this God must be a living God who acts only in love. Peace presupposes an attentiveness at each moment to all that can happen in the heart of a Christian.

Paul, the Apostle, addresses the Ephesians exhorting them to become *sowers of peace*:

"... put away the old self of your former way of life, [they were all pagans] corrupted through deceitful desires, and be renewed in the spirit of your minds, and put on the new self, created in God's way in righteousness and holiness of truth." (Eph 4:24)

Through the Ephesians, Paul tells each one of us:

"Therefore, putting away falsehood, speak the truth, each one to his neighbor, for we are members one of another. Be angry, but do not sin, do not let the sun set on your anger... labor, doing honest work with [your] own hands, in order to have something to share with those in need. No foul language should come out of your mouths but only such as is good for needed edification that it may impart grace to those who hear. And do not grieve the holy Spirit of God with which you were sealed for the day of re-demption. Be attentive to his presence and avoid all bitterness, fury, anger, shouting, and reviling. Be kind to one another, compassionate, forgiving one another as God has forgiven you in Christ." (Eph 4:22-32)

Paul strives to draw people away from paganism to make them sowers of peace. "*Live in a manner worthy of the call you have received.*" (Eph 4:1) We, too, have received this call; it is time that we recognize it. Are we Christians or not? This commitment was taken for us by others but it becomes our responsibility once we have reached the age of reason. Let us for once become aware that this call comes to us from Jesus who chooses his friends and who counts us among the number of his favorites. Let us stop for a moment to tell him that we agree with him, that we accept the challenge, that we are grateful for this call and consider it the chance of a lifetime. That we consciously, freely and voluntarily line up on the side of those who are sowers of peace.

> "Bear with one another through love, strive to preserve the unity of the spirit through the bond of peace: one body and one Spirit, as you were also called to the one hope of your call; one Lord, one faith, one baptism; one God and father of all, who is over all and through all and in all." (Eph 4:2-6)

Our hearts must abide in love, a universal love like that of Jesus. Peace demands that we get rid of egoism, narrow-mindedness, and the mania for passing rash or unfavorable judgements on everyone; that we control our troublesome imaginations, generators of wounded susceptibility.

As the fruit of love, peace requires that we purge ourselves from all the toxins of suffering that on the least occasion burst forth into unhealthy aggressiveness and rid ourselves of all brooding silence that incubates ineradicable bitterness.

Sowers of peace endeavor to live in God, to identify with God, to see him everywhere and in everyone. Peace must permeate and impregnate our whole being if we are to be effective in encouraging people everywhere to establish peace according to their possibilities. We need the genius of certain evangelizers who are able to change the hearts of the powerful throughout the world and to direct their interests to those areas where little people will not be excluded but will feel that they are loved. We cannot give what we do not have. If we are to speak of peace we must prepare peace within ourselves.

Peace is God's treasure that must not be lost. When for the first time Jesus sent out certain of his followers whom he had chosen as his apostles, he invested them with power. He told them the theme they were to announce and sent them out as poor people who possessed none of the earth's riches. He ordered them to accept whatever hospitality was offered them:

> "Whatever town or village you enter, look for a worthy person in it, and stay there until you leave. As you enter a house, wish it peace. If the house is worthy, let your peace come upon it; if not, let your peace return to you. Whoever will not receive you or listen to your words, go outside that house or town and shake the dust from your feet." (Mt 10:11-15)

Peace is a gift of God; it must not be lost. Because of our sensibility and emotivity, we are all exposed to a loss of peace. The Lord tells us that in such circumstances we are to escape, to retain our peace, to shake the dust off our sandals in order to be totally free. If we insist on remaining, we will find it easy to store up bad memories and to fabricate false judgements. Therefore after cleaning all your faculties, flee. The important thing is to remain sowers of peace.

Peace is salvation, liberation and eternal life which enters all homes that welcome it. We would say that the Lord instructed the apostles on the riches of peace. Peace is attachment to our mission; it is unlimited confidence in the commandment of Jesus; it is the solidarity that unites Apostles among themselves; it is the awareness that our actions are guided by the Holy Spirit. None of this must be lost.

4. To Build Peace

Vatican II affirms: "*It is altogether necessary that international institutions cooperate to a better and surer extent and that they be coordinated.*" (Gaudium et Spes, no. 83) After the Council, new organisms for promoting peace sprang up all over the world. Nevertheless, we must ask if we are not seeking only worldly peace. Christians must go beyond that, realizing that as sowers of peace, they must strive to calm agitated nerves, to bring light to distraught minds, to channel dispersed energies and to guide people towards unity.

We do not all have the ability to create organizations, but we can endeavor first of all to bring out the best in ourselves, our family and our work milieu. Each of us can become an animator of peace in the family, in the team, in the community and in society. Each of us can unite ourselves to the Church in order to bring out the best in the parishes, dioceses and communities, which can be marvelously focused organisms of peace. But perhaps they need to be renewed, to examine the quality of their witness or to rebuild their image so that it will be more attractive.

Peace is quite demanding; it needs the actual presence of God. Often, it requires a continuity of concentration. We must admit that peace is not like winning a big lottery prize: we do not receive it once and for all. It is not acquired without attentive efforts; it cannot always resist the daily blows of life. Peace depends on the person in whom it is incarnated; it can have different degrees and suffer fluctuations or misadventures. We must watch over it carefully and attentively each day.

Peace must be cultivated every hour of the day. To make progress is to begin again daily; it is to count our victories and our happy experiences; to share and to be enriched by the lives of others.

We may believe that these five attitudes to be lived daily are an obligation only for priests, religious, members of secular institutes or a few laypeople more specially touched by the grace of conversion. We may think that the presence of God and the recognition that the Holy Spirit lives in the Christian pertain above all to those in cloisters, to the mystics who believe in the spiritual life and in the precise action of God in the universe. We can also believe that these five points can be more or less successfully experimented with by women who are more idoneous to the supernatural heights. In other words, we can believe what we want and act as we see fit because we are endowed with a free will, with a faculty that permits us to make decisions. But the question here is what does Jesus want of his disciples? what does he say in the Gospel? what does he illustrate by his daily behavior?

One thing is certain: he wants us to be *sowers of peace.* There are numerous ways of succeeding; I suggest one which has proved itself efficacious and continues to be efficacious: the way of the five attitudes for meeting Jesus.

1. Presence of God
2. Absence of criticism
3. Absence of complaint
4. Being of service
5. To be a sower of peace.

To succeed in the first four steps which are attitudes of the heart makes us sowers of peace, specialists in the love of our neighbor, adults in faith, imitators of Christ and Mary — his mother and ours. It is as Christians that we are members of the Mystical Body of Christ, that we work for the glory of God, that we become a stabilizing influence for our neighbor, that we take the most effective means for working out our salvation. The indifferent or tepid Christian who neglects thinking of God and referring to him, who acts according to circumstances like an automaton without a goal, who pays little attention to sowing peace is overtaken by spiritual arteriosclerosis, by a spirit of criticism and complaint.

Let us realize that the Lord wants us to preserve the unity of the spirit through the bond of peace (cf. Eph 4:3), that peace is inexplicable and marvelous and surpasses the powers of the intelligence (cf. Phil 4:7). With St. Paul, my wish for you is, that "*the peace of Christ will reign in your hearts,*" (Col 3:15) and "*that you will live in peace with everyone.*" (Rom 12:18) Live in peace and the God of love and peace will be with you. (cf. 2 Cor 13:11) Pursue peace in union with those who call on the Lord with pure minds. (cf. 2 Tm 2:22) In the front lines we find Mary who, to help us find peace, asks us to say to the Lord what she herself said to the angel Gabriel: Here I am to do the will of God. (cf. Lk 1:38) Her Magnificat is the expression of a heart invaded by the Holy Spirit and overflowing with peace.

Perhaps we have the impression that we will never have much success. All the same, what counts is to remain attached to Jesus and to carry out the daily tasks which he asks of us.

Conclusion

Many movements as well as many individuals are seeking practical ways of building up their relationship with God. Without wanting to lay a burden on anyone, I propose that they adopt these five attitudes, or five points: meditate them, learn them by heart. When you read the Bible, you will find their meaning in a multitude of texts, you will see them as basic Biblical attitudes.

You will realize that these five points do not impose any new obligations; they simply want to implant themselves in your faculties like a breath of the Holy Spirit, an ever-watchful energy, a permanent atmosphere of prayer, a tenderness in pursuit of the affection of Jesus, a warm instinct for imitating Mary whom we perceive standing courageously at the foot of the Cross while others flee or break down.

It is undeniable that like the caressing breeze of the desert which Elias recognized as the presence of God, a breath of Pentecost presently covers the whole world. Could not these five points be one means among others to help people who are seeking God, to encourage those have met him and want to remain fervent, or to change and transform the lives of those who are avid for prayer? Many people have been won over to Christ and feel within themselves the inspiration of the Spirit. They perceive that the Lord has given them a heart of flesh, a new spirit, a divine impulse, a supernatural breath. We find these people in the charismatic renewal, the cursillos, the Volunteers of God, Marriage Encounter, in our religious communities, among our priests and in secular institutes. These people want to persevere, to remain fervent, to maintain their enthusiasm, to keep the sacred fire burning, to feel themselves a thought present in the hearts of God and the Virgin.

Therefore, why not try to live these five attitudes which make each of us a disciple of our good Master, sheep belonging to the true Shepherd, a friend whom Jesus knows by name.

I terminate by asking you to meditate this text of St. John (10:22-29):

"The feast of the Dedication (a feast dedicated to the celebration of the victory of Judas Maccabee over Antiochus IV) was then taking place in Jerusalem. It was winter. And Jesus walked about in the temple area on the Portico of Solomon. The Jews gathered round him and said to him: 'How long are you going to keep us in suspense. If you are the Messiah, tell us plainly.' Jesus answered them 'I told you and you do not believe me. The works I do in my Father's name testify to me. But you do not believe, because you are not among my sheep. My sheep hear my voice; I know them and they follow me. I give them eternal life and they shall never perish. No one will take them out of my hands."

Have you noticed that in the last sentence two verbs are in the future tense. The other is in the present indicative tense: I give them eternal life. Is this not true peace, the peace of God which begins immediately here below in the present moment, as soon as we attach ourselves to God by recognizing that he is in us as one who is living and acting. Those who have this awareness are those who listen to him.

Moreover, we comprehend that we are known by Jesus and, because we are beings of service, we truly set out to follow him. To listen and follow — these are the riches that give true peace.

Lord, to love you by living in your presence,
this is what you ask of me.

Lord, to love you by respecting my neighbor,
by finding your presence in him,
by avoiding criticism,
this is what you desire of me.

Lord, to love you by discovering you in my work,
in events, in objects,
by being caught up in the wonder of you,
this is what you desire of me.

Lord, to love you by serving others,
by being your docile instrument,
by surrendering myself totally to you,
this is your plan for me.

Lord, to savor peace,
to be animated by your serenity,
to taste your joy deep within me,
to sense you in my whole being:
this is what I receive from you. Amen

SUR LES PAS DE JÉSUS (1978)
In the Footsteps of Jesus, Éditions Paulines
Sobre las huellas de Jesús, Ediciones MSC
Sulla via del Vangelo, Città Nuova Editrice
Yesuvinte kaladikalil, St. Paul Publications
(To be published in Thaï and German)

JE T'ACCUEILLE (1982)
Yo te Acojo, Ediciones MSC

EN INTIMITÉ AVEC JÉSUS (1987)
En intimidad con Jesús, Ediciones MSC
In Intimacy with Jesus, Éditions Paulines
Intimità con Gesù, Città Nuova Editrice

UN COEUR SUR LA MAIN: Jean Louis Collignon, o.m.i. (1988)

C'EST POSSIBLE DE S'ENTENDRE AVEC LES AUTRES (1978)
Es posible estar de acuerdo con los demás, Ediciones MSC
It Is Possible to Get along with Others!..., Éditions Paulines

LE MOMENT PRÉSENT (1990)
The Present Moment, Éditions Paulines
El Momento Presente, Ediciones MSC
Il momento presente, Città Nuova Editrice

VICTOR LELIÈVRE, un homme branché
  sur le Sacré-Coeur (1993)

Achevé d'imprimer
en août 1993
sur les presses de
Imprimerie H.L.N. Inc.

Imprimé au Canada — Printed in Canada